HOMEMADE DESSERTS

HOMEMADE DESSERTS

Maggie Mayhew
Catherine Atkinson
Caroline Barty

Photography by Ian Garlick

MQP

Published by MQ Publications Limited
12 The Ivories
6-8 Northampton Street
London N1 2HY
Tel: 020 7359 2244
Fax: 020 7359 1616
E-mail: mail@mqpublications.com
www.mqpublications.com

North American office
49 West 24th Street
8th Floor
New York, NY 10010
E-mail: information@mqpublicationsus.com

Copyright © 2006 MQ Publications Limited
Recipes: Catherine Atkinson, Caroline Barty, Maggie Mayhew
Photography: Ian Garlick
Home Economy: Alice Hart
Illustrations: Penny Brown

ISBN: 1-84601-145-0
978-1-84601-145-0

1 3 5 7 9 0 8 6 4 2

Printed in China

IMPORTANT: Those who might be at risk from the effects of salmonella
poisoning (the elderly, pregnant women, young children and those suffering
from immune deficiency diseases) should consult their GP with any concerns
about eating raw eggs.

Contents

Introduction

There is always room for a bit of dessert. Whether it is your grandma's secret recipe apple pie, a naughty chocolate treat shared with a friend, or the amazing concoction presented by your host at a dinner party, everyone loves a homemade dish. As we were growing up, many of our moms and grandmothers wouldn't have dreamed of buying a prepackaged dessert to round off a meal. Now that mass-market brands have made this type of ready-made food available, and since many more of us work full-time, we seem to have hung up our aprons for good. We see a layered cake or a colorful trifle at the supermarket and think we could never make it ourselves. But baking a pie or whipping up a fruity mousse can be one of the most enjoyable ends to a day in the office, and it's something the whole family can get involved with—and enjoy the results.

Split into six chapters—Grandma's Best, Chocolate Heaven, Cool & Creamy, Pies & Tarts, Fruity Favorites, and Dinner Party Delights—*Homemade Desserts* guides you through each recipe step-by-step, providing helpful tips on preparation techniques, serving suggestions, and storage advice along the way. A comprehensive introduction takes you through the basics, providing you with the skills needed to produce stunning desserts, from beautifully turned out pastry to deliciously smooth ice cream. Start out simple with recipes like Fried Bananas with Rum & Brown Sugar or Spiced Baked Apples, and as you gain more confidence try your hand at more complicated recipes like Freeform Strawberry Rhubarb Pie and Pavlova with Tropical Fruits. Making your own food is the best way to control what you eat, and *Homemade Desserts* shows you how to make the most out of fresh and wholesome ingredients.

The recipes that follow will win back your enthusiasm for the kitchen, as well as encourage all the family to eat well and to eat together. Every recipe is an achievable goal, so rise to the challenge, and wow your next group of dinner guests with a scrumptious soufflé, tower of profiteroles, or fruity meringue. If you haven't baked since you were in high school, start with easy recipes and try to make something different once a week. After a few months everyone will have a favorite, and you will be inundated with requests. Don't worry if your first few attempts are a bit shaky—that's the beauty of a homemade dessert, even the raw ingredients taste good. Remember licking the spoon when you were growing up? Enjoying your mistakes is all part of the learning curve. As your confidence grows you will find yourself swapping pastry tips, and have found a few of your own secret ingredients.

Dessert Techniques & Tips

THE BASICS

Whipping cream

It is important to start with chilled cream—either heavy or whipping cream—and use a cold bowl, preferably ceramic, stainless steel or glass. The best style of beater to use is a balloon whisk, hand-held electric mixer, or old-fashioned hand-held rotary egg beater. Whip quickly to begin with until the cream starts to thicken and becomes the consistency of custard. Now's the time to reduce the whipping speed so you don't over whip. If you continue whipping for a short while, the cream will begin to hold its shape but will drop easily from a spoon. At this stage it is of spooning consistency. It will have some texture but won't hold its shape for long.

If you whip for a few seconds more, the cream should start to hold its shape and will have a glossy sheen. Once you get to this stage, the cream is perfect for serving, as it will thicken slightly on standing or piping.

Make sure you don't over whip your cream. If you keep whipping past this stage, the cream will form stiff peaks and become too thick and buttery in texture. If over-whipped cream is left at room temperature it may even separate out into curds and whey.

Beating egg whites

Beating is a vital process in the making of a meringue. When egg whites are beaten, they increase their volume and become frothy, light, and airy. They will achieve a better volume if they are left at room temperature for a couple of hours, and not used cold, straight from the refrigerator.

Use a balloon whisk for the best volume and texture, but if you are not used to beating by hand, or speed is of the essence, an electric hand-held or standing mixer will be fine. Separate the eggs, allowing the whites to drop into a grease-free, non-reactive bowl. If any egg yolk falls in with it, remove before starting to beat. The easiest way to do this is to use one of the broken eggshells: for some quirky reason the yolk is attracted to the shell. Beat quickly and lightly in an even, steady movement. The egg whites will become frothy but still liquid.

If you continue beating past this stage the egg whites will become stiff but smooth. This is the stiff peak stage, when sugar or syrup can be added. A good way to check if this stage has been reached is to tip the bowl. If the egg whites begin to slide out of the bowl they need further beating.

If sugar is to be added, lightly sprinkle it over the top, a spoonful at a time, beating well in between each addition. When the egg whites are very stiff and glossy the remaining sugar or ingredients can be folded in gently with a metal spoon to prevent knocking out the air.

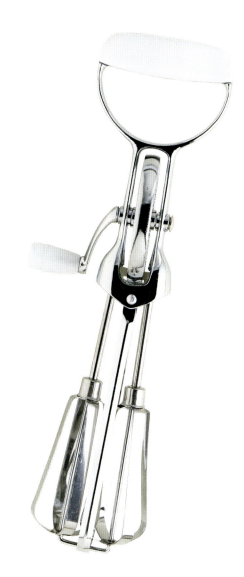

TIPS FOR SUCCESSFUL PIE MAKING

Equipment

Using the correct baking equipment simplifies and enhances pie making, but few specialist implements are essential. You probably already possess the basic items: standard measuring cups and spoons or accurate weighing scales, a large glass measuring cup, a good-sized mixing bowl, a fine strainer, and a few sharp knives. Other important items include:

ROLLING PIN
A thick, heavy one is best for rolling out dough, although marble rolling pins are cooler.

TIMER
Vital when making pies.

PIE PLATES AND DISHES
In glass or porcelain, which have an unglazed base to allow heat to penetrate. These are especially useful for single-crust pies.

TART PANS
The best are metal with fluted sides, which are easier to line. Loose bases will simplify removal.

PASTRY BRUSH
For even glazing.

BAKING BEANS
For "baking blind." Choose ceramic or aluminum ones, which last forever and are food heat conductors, or simply use dried beans.

WIRE RACK
To allow air to circulate and prevent sogginess when cooling pie crusts.

PIE PANS AND DISHES
When deciding on which pan to use it is best to be led by the recipe. For an open pie or tart, recipes usually call for a metal loose-bottomed tart pan. These are generally favored above china ones because they conduct heat more efficiently—the last thing you want is a soggy, undercooked crust! Loose-bottomed pans also allow the pie to be transferred easily onto a serving plate, which makes it a lot easier to slice. It's also worth investing in good old-fashioned shallow and deep pie dishes. The gentle sloping sides make lining the dishes easy and the pastry won't slip down if you're blind baking. Finally, remember that if you change the dish size from the recipe you will have to adjust the cooking times: a smaller, deeper pie will take longer to cook than a shallow, wide one.

Ingredients

Most pastry doughs are created from three simple ingredients: flour, shortening, and water. Used in the correct proportions and handled correctly, these make delicious, flaky pie crusts. The addition of egg or egg yolk, sweetener, and flavoring are ways of altering the taste and texture of the final product.

Traditional pastry calls for all-purpose flour, and no other type should be used unless specified in the recipe. Self-rising flour produces softer pastry and may be used in a lard-crust. Whole-wheat flour makes a much heavier dough, but it is sometimes used together with white flour. Pastry can be made with one fat or a mixture. Butter on its own gives an excellent flavor and color. If margarine is preferred it should be the hard-stick variety. Shortening makes more flaky pastry and is often used with butter in equal amounts.

Making perfect pastry

There are many different types of crusts, from buttery, layered puff, and flaky pastry to paper-thin filo, also known as strudel pastry. Shortcrust is probably the best known and most frequently used for pie making. While it's the simplest of all pastries, it needs a cool, light hand and you should avoid overhandling the dough or it will become tough.

PASTRY METHODS
MANUAL VS. FOOD PROCESSOR
Throughout this book you will find different methods for making dough. Some require the rubbing-in method, others tell you to use the food processor. If you don't like getting your hands dirty you can use the food processor all the time but, to my mind, the best, lightest crust is made by the hands-on method. The main thing to remember is to keep the butter and water cold and not to overwork the dough. Go easy when adding the water—too much and you will end up with tough pastry. You can tell how much water to add by feeling the texture of the dough.

Shortcrust dough: the basic method

There is a great deal of mystique surrounding the making of shortcrust dough. In fact, the method is very straightforward and just takes a little practice. If you're worried that your hands are too warm to rub the butter in as described below, try using two knives to cut the butter into small pieces. Rest the dough before rolling or it may shrink on cooking, producing an uneven result.

To make enough shortcrust dough to line a 9-inch flan pan, you'll need 1¾ cups all-purpose flour, a pinch salt, 6 tablespoons cold butter, diced, and 2–3 tablespoons cold water.

STEP 1

Sift the flour into a mixing bowl with the salt. Add the butter and using your fingertips, rub or cut the butter into the flour until the mixture resembles coarse breadcrumbs.

STEP 2

Add 2 tablespoons of the water and using your hands, start to bring the dough together, adding a little more water if necessary. Do not use too much water or the resulting pastry will be tough.

STEP 3

Turn the dough onto a lightly floured surface and knead briefly, just until the dough is smooth. Form into a ball, flatten into a disc, and wrap in plastic wrap. Chill at least 30 minutes.

STEP 4

Remove the dough from the refrigerator. Unwrap and put onto a lightly floured surface. Lightly flour the top of the dough under the rolling pin while rolling it back and forth. Try not to stretch the dough by pulling—allow the weight and pressure of the pin to roll the dough.

STEP 5

Roll the dough into a rough circle at least 2 inches in diameter larger than a loose-bottomed 9-inch fluted flan pan. Gently roll the dough onto the rolling pin, then unroll it over the pan to cover. Carefully press the pastry into the edge of the pan, removing any overhanging pastry with a knife.

STEP 6

Prick the base all over with a fork, being careful not to make holes right through the dough. This helps to keep the dough from rising in the middle during baking. Chill 20 minutes.

Rough puff pastry: the basic method

This is an unusual method for making rough puff pastry, as the dough includes baking powder and is bound with buttermilk. This helps to give the pastry a good rise as well as an excellent flavor. This dough can be frozen, well wrapped, for up to 2 months. Allow to thaw completely before using. See the recipe on page 14 to prepare the basic rough dough pastry.

1 Sift the flour, salt, baking powder, and baking soda into a mixing bowl. Cut the butter into dice, add to the flour, and rub together using your fingertips until the mixture resembles very coarse breadcrumbs. The pieces of butter should still be discernible, but all coated in flour.

2 Follow steps 1, 2, and 3 (see p.14).

3 Transfer the dough to a baking sheet or tray lined with parchment paper. Cover with plastic wrap and chill, about 20 minutes.

4 Remove from the refrigerator and repeat the rolling and folding twice more. Prepare to this point if using to top a pie or for use in the recipe that follows.

STEP 1

Stir in about half the buttermilk and begin mixing the dough together, adding just enough of the remaining buttermilk to make a soft dough.

STEP 2

Turn the dough onto a floured surface and dust with flour as well. Roll the dough out to 1-inch thick. Lift the dough from the surface and fold it, like a letter, in thirds.

STEP 3

Give the dough a quarter turn. Flour the surface and dough again and reroll the dough into a rectangle, of the same thickness. Repeat the folding and turning.

Rolling out technique

This is often the part that puts people off making their own puff pastry. The first thing to remember is to rest the dough—nine times out of ten if someone is having trouble rolling out puff pastry it is because they skipped the resting period. Resting is essential as the gluten in the flour reacts with liquid and becomes elastic and pliable over time. This will make the dough easier to roll out and less liable to tear or crumble. Wrap the pastry in plastic wrap and leave in the refrigerator for at least 20 minutes. When you take it out of the refrigerator allow it to rest at room temperature for 5 to 10 minutes to soften a little. Shape the dough with your hands into the shape of the pan you are using. So if you are using a rectangular pan roughly shape the dough into a rectangle—this just makes it easier to roll out into the right proportions. Don't turn the pastry during rolling—there is a chance it will tear and shrink too much.

Lining a tart pan

1 On a lightly floured surface, roll out the dough to a thickness of ⅛ inch and to a circle about 2 to 3 inches larger than the tart pan, depending on the depth of the pan.

2 Lift the dough with the rolling pin and ease it into the pan. Press the pastry against the side of the pan so that there are no gaps. Roll the rolling pin over the top of the pan to cut off the excess dough.

3 Prick the base of the dough liberally, and then chill for at least 10 minutes, to prevent puffing and shrinkage during baking.

Baking blind

This is used either to partly cook an empty pie shell, so that is does not become soggy when the filling is added, or to completely bake a pie shell when the filling isn't baked.

1 To bake the pie shell partially, cover the pastry with parchment paper or foil and fill with dried or baking beans. Bake at 400°F for 10 to 15 minutes. Remove the paper or foil and beans. Brush with beaten egg, if the filling is moist, to seal the base. Bake for 5 minutes more.

2 To fully bake the pie shell, follow the above, but bake for 10 minutes after the paper or foil are removed, or until golden brown. Cool before filling.

Keeping and freezing pastry

Uncooked pie dough, puff pastry dough, and most other pastry doughs can be stored chilled for several days in plastic wrap to prevent them from drying out. Dough may also be frozen for several weeks;

thaw in the refrigerator overnight, then leave at room temperature for 15 minutes before rolling out. You can also freeze sheets of rolled out dough, placed on parchment paper on a baking sheet and covered with plastic wrap. Unbaked pie shells will keep covered in the refrigerator for 2 to 3 days, or for a week in the freezer. Fully baked pie shells may be frozen or kept in an airtight container for a day or two.

Baking tips

- Always bake pie shells and double-crust pies on a heated baking sheet. This helps to crisp the pie crust and also catch any drips should the filled shell or pie start to bubble over.
- If you find any small holes in a cooked pie shell, repair them by brushing with beaten egg, then return to the oven for 2 to 3 minutes to seal.
- If the pastry has fully browned before the filling is cooked, protect it with foil. Cover single and double-crust pies completely, making a hole in the foil to let steam escape. On open pie shells, cover the pastry edge only with strips of foil.

TIPS FOR SUCCESSFUL ICE CREAM & FROZEN DESSERTS

Below are some tips and tricks to perfect frozen desserts.

- Ice cream is best when stored between -5°F and 0°F.

- Never let ice cream melt and refreeze. It won't look too appetizing.

- The faster the ice cream freezes, the smoother the texture.

- Create mixtures for churn-frozen ice creams the day before you freeze, to increase yield and produce a smoother texture.

- Make sure ice cream is covered so that it does not absorb flavors from other foods.

- As a rule, fill the churn/machine no more than two-thirds full to allow room for expansion.

- Allow 5–6 quarts of chipped or cracked ice to ½ pound of coarse rock salt for old-fashioned machines, and let the ice stand for 3 minutes before beginning.

- For hand-crank machines, begin with a slow crank, about 40 turns per minute until you feel the mixture begin to thicken by resistance. Then triple your speed for 5–6 minutes. Add any chopped fruit after this step before repacking the salt ice and finishing with about 80 turns per minute for another few minutes to finish.

- Overfilling the inner container with the ice cream mixture, too much salt in the ice-packing mixture, and/or churning too rapidly can result in a granular texture.

- For ices, use no more than 1 part sugar to 4 parts liquid. The ice will not freeze properly if there is too much sugar. The larger the proportion of sugar or other sweetener, the slower the mixture freezes. Any alcohol should be added after the ice has frozen.

- Whipped cream or evaporated milk, melted marshmallows, beaten eggs, gelatin and other ingredients are all additives used to prevent the formation of large ice crystals as well as improve or vary flavor. A tip to avoid ice crystals: add 1 envelope of unflavored gelatin per 6 cups of ice cream mixture. Let the gelatin soften in ¼ cup of the mixture, then gently heat it until it is dissolved. Add to the remaining mixture and proceed.

- After your ice cream is done, let it sit in the freezer for four hours before eating it to let it develop flavor and texture.

Ice cream: the basic method

An ice cream base is made by combining a custard mixture with whipped cream. It's frozen for short bursts and whisked to break down the ice crystals formed during freezing. To make about 1 quart of vanilla ice cream, you will need a generous cup of whole milk, ½ vanilla bean, 2 egg yolks, 4 tablespoons granulated sugar, and 2¼ cups heavy cream.

STEP 1

Bring the milk and vanilla bean to simmering point over low heat. Remove the pan from the heat then remove the vanilla bean. Whisk the egg yolks and sugar with a hand-held electric mixer until pale and slightly thickened. Gently mix in the hot milk.

STEP 2

Pour into a heavy-based pan. Cook over a low heat, stirring constantly until the mixture thickens to the consistency of heavy cream and coats the back of the spoon.

STEP 3

Tear off some plastic wrap and then press down over the surface of the custard (this will stop a skin from forming) and set to one side to go cold.

STEP 4

Pour the cream into a bowl. Using a hand-held electric mixer, whip the cream until it forms stiff peaks. When the custard is cold, fold in the cream.

STEP 5

Pour into a freezer container and freeze until half-frozen. Whisk to break up the ice crystals then return to the freezer. Repeat twice more until thick. Stir in the flavorings and, finally freeze until firm. Alternatively, churn in an ice cream maker.

GRANDMA'S BEST

- *Pumpkin Pie*
- *Shoofly Pie*
- *Sweet Raisin Pie*
- *Four Berry Pie*
- *Fruity Bread & Butter Pudding*
- *Sticky Toffee Pudding*
- *Black Currant Pie*
- *Peach & Raspberry Pies*
- *Peach Tart*
- *Sweet Potato Pie*
- *Eggnog Tart*
- *Apple Strudel*
- *Sweet Vanilla Soufflé*
- *Black Cherry & Chocolate Cake*
- *Cherry Cinnamon Cobbler*

- *Grape Pie*
- *Deep-Dish Apple Pie à la Mode*
- *Banoffee Pie*
- *Two-Crust Prune Pie*
- *Peach Cobbler*
- *Cranberry Pie*
- *Key Lime Pie*
- *Blackberry & Apple Pie*
- *Cherry Strudel*
- *Linzertorte with a Lattice Top*
- *Hot Waffles & Banana with Toffee Brandy Sauce*
- *Jelly Roll with Lemon Cream*
- *Crumb Pie*
- *Baked Apples with Walnut Jackets*
- *Banana & Toffee Cheesecake*

CHAPTER ONE

GRANDMA'S BEST

Pumpkin Pie

Serves 6–8

2¾ cups all-purpose flour, plus extra
   for dusting
Pinch of salt
1½ sticks (12 tablespoons) cold butter
4–5 tablespoons water
Light cream, to serve

For the filling

2 cups freshly-cooked or canned
   pumpkin or squash purée
2 eggs, beaten
½ cup packed brown sugar
1 cup light corn syrup
1 cup heavy cream
2 teaspoons ground cinnamon
1 teaspoon ground ginger
½ teaspoon freshly grated nutmeg
1 teaspoon pure vanilla extract

1 Sift the flour and salt into a mixing bowl. Add the butter and rub it in until the mixture resembles bread crumbs. Add 4 tablespoons cold water and mix to a firm dough, adding more water, if necessary. Knead until smooth. Wrap in plastic wrap and chill for 20 minutes.

2 Roll out the dough on a lightly floured surface into a rough round at least 2 inches larger than a loose-bottomed 12-inch fluted tart pan. Line the pan and trim off any excess dough. Prick the base all over. Chill for 20 minutes. Put a baking sheet in the oven and preheat to 400°F.

3 Line the pie shell with parchment paper and fill with baking beans. Bake for 20 minutes. Remove the paper and beans. Reduce the oven temperature to 375°F.

4 Add the eggs, sugar, corn syrup, and cream to the pumpkin purée and mix. Stir in the spices and vanilla extract. Spoon the mixture into the pie shell and bake for 30–35 minutes, or until set. Serve warm with cream.

Shoofly Pie

Serves 6–8

1⅓ cups all-purpose flour, plus extra
    for dusting
Pinch of salt
¾ stick (6 tablespoons) cold butter, diced
About 2 tablespoons cold water
Light cream, to serve

For the filling
2 eggs, lightly beaten
¾ cup plus 2 tablespoons all-purpose
    flour
½ cup packed dark brown sugar
¼ teaspoon each ground ginger and
    grated nutmeg
½ teaspoon ground cinnamon
⅔ stick (5 tablespoons) butter, diced
¾ cup molasses
6 tablespoons boiling water
½ teaspoon baking soda

1 Sift the flour and salt into a mixing bowl. Add the butter and rub it in until the mixture resembles fine bread crumbs. Sprinkle the water over the flour mixture, and stir to make a firm dough. Knead briefly, then form into a neat ball, wrap in plastic wrap, and chill for 30 minutes. Put a baking sheet in the oven and preheat to 400°F.

2 Roll out the dough on a lightly floured surface and use to line a 9-inch pie pan. Trim and flute the edges, then prick the base all over with a fork. Chill for 15 minutes.

3 Line the pie dough with parchment paper and fill with baking beans. Bake blind for 15 minutes. Remove the paper and beans, brush the base with 1 teaspoon beaten egg from the filling, and bake for 5 minutes. Remove from the oven and reduce the temperature to 375°F.

4 For the filling, sift the flour into a bowl. Stir in the brown sugar and spices. Rub in the butter until the mixture resembles coarse bread crumbs. Sprinkle a third in the pie shell.

5 Beat the eggs and molasses together in a bowl. Pour the boiling water into a glass measuring cup and stir in the baking soda (it will froth up, so make sure there's room for this). Immediately pour into the egg mixture and beat together.

6 Quickly pour the mixture into the pie shell and sprinkle evenly with the remaining spice mixture. Bake for 30–35 minutes, or until firm and browned. Serve warm or at room temperature with custard or cream.

Sweet Raisin Pie

Serves 8–10

1⅓ cups all-purpose flour, plus extra
  for dusting
1 stick (8 tablespoons) cold butter, diced
2 teaspoons sugar
1 egg, lightly beaten

For the filling
1 stick (8 tablespoons) butter
1 cup packed light brown sugar
1 teaspoon ground cinnamon
½ teaspoon ground allspice
Pinch of freshly grated nutmeg
4 egg yolks
2 tablespoons all-purpose flour
1 cup heavy cream
½ cup raisins
½ cup chopped dates
⅔ cup chopped pecans

1 Sift the flour into a bowl. Add the butter and rub it in until the mixture resembles bread crumbs. Stir in the sugar, add all but 2 teaspoons of the beaten egg and mix to a firm dough. Knead briefly, then form into a neat ball, wrap in plastic wrap and chill for 30 minutes.

2 Put a baking sheet in the oven and preheat to 400°F. Roll out the dough on a lightly floured surface and use to line a shallow 9-inch pie pan. Prick the base all over with a fork then chill for 10 minutes.

3 Line the pie shell with parchment paper and fill with baking beans. Bake blind for 15 minutes. Remove the paper and beans and bake for 5 minutes. Reduce the oven temperature to 325°F.

4 For the filling, cream the butter, sugar, and spices together in a bowl until light then beat in the egg yolks, one at a time. Sift over the flour and beat in, then stir in the cream, raisins, dates, and nuts.

5 Spoon the filling into the pie shell and bake for 30 minutes, or until lightly set. Cool for 10 minutes, then serve warm.

Four Berry Pie

Serves 6

2⅓ cups all-purpose flour, plus extra
  for dusting
1 tablespoon sugar
1 teaspoon grated orange zest
1½ sticks (12 tablespoons) cold butter,
  diced
2½–3 tablespoons cold water
Whipped cream, to serve

For the filling
2 cups raspberries
1½ cups blackberries
1 cup blueberries
1 cup strawberries, hulled and
  quartered
¼ cup granulated sugar, or to taste
1 tablespoon cornstarch
Beaten egg, for glazing
1 tablespoon confectioners' sugar

1 Sift the flour and sugar into a mixing bowl, then stir in the orange zest. Add the butter and rub it in until the mixture resembles fine bread crumbs. Sprinkle over 2½ tablespoons of the water and mix to a firm dough, adding the remaining water if needed. Wrap in plastic wrap and chill for 30 minutes.

2 To make the filling, put the fruit into a bowl with the strawberries at the top, then sprinkle over the sugar. After a few minutes, toss the fruit with your hands. Leave for 20 minutes. Meanwhile, put a baking sheet in the oven and preheat to 400°F.

3 Roll out two-thirds of the dough on a lightly floured surface to a round about 1½ inches larger all round than a shallow 8–9-inch pie pan. Line the pan, leaving an overhang of dough, and then dampen the edge with a little water.

4 Carefully transfer the fruit to the pie shell using your hands. Blend the cornstarch and the fruit juice at the bottom of the bowl together to form a smooth paste, and drizzle this over the fruit.

5 Roll out the remaining dough to make a lid and use to cover the pie, pressing the edges together well to seal. Trim the excess dough with a knife. Crimp the edge of the pie and make decorations from the re-rolled dough trimmings.

6 Brush the pie with beaten egg to glaze, then sprinkle with confectioners' sugar. Slash the top twice or make small holes with a skewer to allow steam to escape. Bake for 35–45 minutes, or until the crust is a deep golden brown. Cool for 10 minutes before serving with whipped cream.

Fruity Bread & Butter Pudding

Serves 8

⅔ stick (5 tablespoons) unsalted butter,
  softened, plus extra for greasing
1¼ cups milk
1¼ cups heavy cream
1 vanilla bean, split
About 6 slices day-old white bread,
  crusts removed
2 tablespoons apricot jam
2 tablespoons dried apricots, chopped
1 tablespoon dark raisins
2 tablespoons golden raisins
6 egg yolks
¼ cup granulated sugar
Light cream, to serve

Tip
Make a number of delicious versions by substituting the white bread with croissants, brioche, panettone, or French bread.

1 Preheat the oven to 350°F. Lightly grease a shallow 6-cup ovenproof dish.

2 Put the milk, cream, and vanilla bean into a saucepan and heat gently until simmering. Remove from heat and leave to infuse for 15 minutes.

3 Butter the bread generously. Spread half the slices with the apricot jam. Cut each slice into 4 triangles and use the bread spread with jam to line the base of the dish. Scatter the apricots and raisins over the bread in the dish. Arrange the remaining bread triangles attractively on top.

4 Meanwhile, whisk the egg yolks and sugar together until pale and creamy. Strain the milk and cream mixture on to the egg yolks and sugar, whisking all the time. Carefully pour the custard mixture over the bread as evenly as possible. Press the bread gently into the custard. Set aside for 20–30 minutes.

5 Transfer the dish to the oven and bake for 30–35 minutes until the custard is just set and the bread is golden and crisp on top. Serve warm with cream.

Sticky Toffee Pudding

Serves 2

¹/₃ stick (3 tablespoons) butter,
softened, plus extra for greasing
¼ cup packed brown sugar
1 egg, beaten
¾ cup self-rising flour
⅓ cup chopped dates
2 tablespoons milk

For the sauce
⅓ cup packed brown sugar
½ cup heavy cream
3 tablespoons butter

1 Grease a 1-quart pudding basin. Beat the butter and sugar together in a separate bowl until light and fluffy, then beat in the egg a little at a time. Fold in the flour, then stir in the dates and enough of the milk to give the mixture a soft, dropping consistency.

2 Spoon the mixture into the prepared pudding basin. Cut a round of parchment paper and a round of foil about 2 inches larger than the top of the basin, and grease the bottom of the paper. Place both over the bowl and secure with string.

3 Put the bowl in a large saucepan and pour boiling water around the bowl, to come two-thirds of the way up the sides. Cover and simmer for 1–1½ hours until risen and springy when pressed. Check the water occasionally, topping up if necessary.

4 Put all the sauce ingredients in a small saucepan and heat gently, stirring, until combined. Simmer for 5 minutes, or until thickened. Turn the pudding out on to a plate and serve with the sauce.

Huckleberry Pie

Serves 6

¼ cup all-purpose flour, plus extra for dusting
⅓ cup whole-wheat flour
Pinch of salt
½ stick (4 tablespoons) cold butter, diced
1 teaspoon grated orange zest
2 tablespoons cold water
Beaten egg, for glazing
1 tablespoon raw sugar, for sprinkling
Custard or cream, to serve

For the filling

2 pounds huckleberries
⅓ cup sugar, or to taste
2 tablespoons cornstarch, sifted
Juice of ½ small orange
1 tablespoon butter

1 Sift the flours and salt into a bowl. Add the bran left in the sieve, then add the butter and rub it in until the mixture resembles bread crumbs. Stir in the orange zest, then sprinkle the water over the dry ingredients and mix to a firm dough. Knead, wrap in plastic wrap, and chill for 30 minutes.

2 Tip the huckleberries into a large bowl. Mix the sugar and cornstarch together and sprinkle over the huckleberries. Squeeze over the orange juice, then toss together. Let stand for 10 minutes.

3 Preheat the oven to 400°F. Using an inverted 9-inch pie pan as a guide, roll out the dough on a floured surface until it is 2 inches larger all round than the dish. Cut a 1-inch strip from around the edge. Moisten the rim of the dish and position the strip on the rim. Brush with water.

4 Spoon the filling into the dish, mounding it in the center. Dot the top with butter. Place the dough lid on top, seal and crimp the edges, and snip a hole in the top to allow steam to escape. Brush with beaten egg and sprinkle with raw sugar.

5 Bake for 20 minutes, reduce the temperature to 350°F, then bake for 15–25 minutes, or until the crust is lightly browned and crisp. Serve with custard or cream.

Peach & Raspberry Pies

Serves 4

1¾ cups all-purpose flour, plus extra
    for dusting
Pinch of salt
1 stick (8 tablespoons) cold butter,
    diced
3–4 tablespoons cold water

For the filling
4 large ripe peaches, pitted and
    roughly chopped
1 cup raspberries
⅓ cup granulated sugar, plus extra for
    sprinkling
Juice of ½ lemon
1 tablespoon milk, for glazing
Crème fraîche or sour cream, to serve

1 Sift the flour and salt into a mixing bowl.
Add the butter and rub it in until the mixture
resembles coarse bread crumbs. Add 2 tablespoons
water and using your hands, start to bring
the dough together, adding a little more water
if necessary. Knead, then form the dough into a neat
ball, wrap in plastic wrap and chill for 30 minutes.

2 Mix the peaches, raspberries, sugar, and lemon
juice together in a bowl and set aside.

3 Preheat the oven to 400°F. Divide the dough
into 4 equal portions. Working with one portion
at a time, divide into one-third and two-thirds. Roll
out the larger piece to fit a 4-inch tartlet pan. Add a
quarter of the peach mixture. Wet the edges of the
dough and roll out the smaller portion of dough.
Use to top the pie, trimming off the excess and
crimping the edges to seal. Snip a hole in the top
of the pie to allow steam to escape.

4 Brush the dough edges with a little milk and
sprinkle with granulated sugar. Repeat to make
4 pies. Transfer the pies to the oven and bake for
about 20–25 minutes, or until the crust is golden.

5 Let cool for about 10 minutes, then carefully
turn the pies out of their pans. Serve with
crème fraîche or sour cream.

Peach Cake

Makes 10–12 slices

1½ sticks (12 tablespoons) unsalted
  butter, softened
1 cup granulated sugar
3 eggs, beaten
2 cups ground almonds
⅔ cup self-rising flour
2 teaspoons pure vanilla extract
One 15-ounce can peach halves in fruit
  juice, drained
Sifted confectioners' sugar, to dust

1 Preheat the oven to 350°F. Grease and line a deep 9-inch round cake pan.

2 Cream the butter and sugar together in a bowl until pale and fluffy, then gradually add the eggs, beating well after each addition. Stir in the ground almonds, flour, and vanilla extract.

3 Spoon the mixture into the prepared pan and smooth the surface. Arrange the peach halves, cut-side down, over the top.

4 Bake in the oven for 35–40 minutes, or until risen and golden brown. Cool in the pan for 10 minutes, then turn out onto a wire rack, invert the cake so that the peaches are on top and let cool completely. Dust with the sifted confectioners' sugar. Serve in slices.

Sweet Potato Pie

Serves 6–8

1½ cups all-purpose flour, plus extra
for dusting
Pinch of salt
¾ stick (6 tablespoons) cold butter,
diced
2 tablespoons cold water
Light cream, to serve

For the filling
1¾ pounds sweet potatoes, peeled and
cut into large chunks
1 cup light cream
2 eggs, lightly beaten
3 tablespoons butter, softened
¼ cup packed light brown sugar
½ teaspoon ground cinnamon
½ teaspoon ground ginger
¼ teaspoon freshly grated nutmeg
1 teaspoon pure vanilla extract

1 Sift the flour and salt into a bowl. Add the butter and rub it in until the mixture resembles fine bread crumbs. Sprinkle over the water and mix to a dough. Knead, then wrap and chill for 30 minutes.

2 Put a baking sheet in the oven and preheat to 400°F. Roll out the dough on a floured surface and use to line a 9-inch tart pan. Prick the base all over then chill for 10 minutes.

3 Put the sweet potatoes in a non-stick roasting pan, cover with foil and roast for 30 minutes, or until soft. Remove, and while warm, mash them in a bowl until very smooth with a few spoonfuls of the cream. About halfway through the potatoes' cooking time, line the tart shell with parchment paper and fill with baking beans. Bake for 15 minutes, remove the paper and beans, brush with 1 teaspoon beaten egg from the filling, and bake for a further 5 minutes. Reduce the temperature to 350°F.

4 Cream the butter and sugar together in a bowl until light. Gradually beat in the eggs, then stir in the spices and vanilla. Stir the remaining cream into the mashed sweet potato until mixed. Spoon into the tart shell. Bake for 40–45 minutes, or until lightly browned. Serve with cream.

Eggnog Tart

Serves 6–8

2 cups all-purpose flour, plus extra
   for dusting
Pinch of salt
$^2/_3$ stick (5 tablespoons) cold unsalted
   butter, diced
$^1/_4$ cup shortening
2–3 tablespoons cold water

For the filling
4 eggs, separated
$^1/_2$ cup granulated sugar
1 cup Dutch Advocaat liqueur or
   Mexican rompope
1$^1/_4$ cups light cream
$^1/_4$ cup boiling water
1 tablespoon powdered gelatin
Soft fruit, such as blackberries,
   raspberries or strawberries,
   to decorate (optional)

1 Sift the flour and salt into a mixing bowl. Add the butter and shortening and rub it in until the mixture resembles coarse bread crumbs. Add 2 tablespoons water and using your hands, bring the dough together, adding a little more water if necessary. Knead briefly, then wrap in plastic wrap and chill for 30 minutes.

2 Roll out the dough on a lightly floured surface and use to line a loose-bottomed 9-inch tart pan. Prick the dough with a fork and chill for 10 minutes.

3 Preheat the oven to 375°F. Line the tart shell with parchment paper and fill with baking beans. Bake blind for 20 minutes. Remove the paper and beans and cook for a further 5 minutes. Let cool completely.

4 For the filling, beat the egg yolks, sugar, and liqueur together in a bowl. Bring the cream to a boil in a nonstick saucepan. Pour the cream over the egg yolks and mix well. Return to the pan and stir over a low heat until the sauce thickens enough to coat the back of a spoon. Remove from the heat.

5 Pour the boiling water into a small bowl. Sprinkle over the gelatin and stir well until dissolved. Pour into the custard mixture and mix well. Leave the custard to cool, then chill until thickened and on the point of setting.

6 Whisk the egg whites in a clean, grease-free bowl until stiff peaks form, then fold into the custard. Pour the mixture into the tart shell and level out. Chill for a further 30 minutes then decorate with soft fruit.

Apple Strudel

Serves 8

6 large sheets of phyllo pastry, about
  2 ounces, thawed if frozen
$1/3$ stick (3 tablespoons) butter, melted,
  plus extra for greasing
2 tablespoons confectioners' sugar,
  for dusting
Sour cream or crème fraîche, to serve

For the filling
$1\frac{1}{2}$ pounds (about 7) Golden Delicious
  or other eating apples
$\frac{1}{2}$ cup raisins
Grated zest and juice of $\frac{1}{2}$ lemon
$\frac{1}{4}$ cup fresh white bread crumbs
3 tablespoons granulated sugar
$\frac{1}{2}$ teaspoon ground cinnamon

1 Remove the phyllo pastry from the refrigerator and leave, still in its wrapping, at room temperature for 20 minutes.

2 Meanwhile, peel, core and thinly slice the apples. Put them in a bowl with the raisins and lemon zest. Sprinkle with the lemon juice and toss to coat. Add the bread crumbs, sugar, and cinnamon, and mix again.

3 Preheat the oven to 375°F and grease a large baking sheet. Lay one sheet of phyllo pastry on a slightly damp kitchen towel, and lightly brush with melted butter. Place a second sheet on top. Continue to layer the phyllo, brushing butter between each sheet.

4 Spoon the apple mixture over the phyllo pastry leaving a 1-inch margin around the edges. Turn in the short pastry edges. With the help of the kitchen towel, roll up from a long edge to completely enclose the filling.

5 Transfer the strudel to the prepared baking sheet, seam-side down. Brush with butter and bake for 35–40 minutes until the apples are soft. If necessary, cover the strudel loosely with foil to prevent overbrowning. Dust with confectioners' sugar and serve hot with sour cream or crème fraîche.

Sweet Vanilla Soufflé

Serves 6

1¼ cups milk
1 vanilla bean, split
½ cup granulated sugar, plus extra for
  sprinkling
⅓ stick (3 tablespoons) butter, plus
  extra for greasing
⅓ cup all-purpose flour
3 large eggs, separated
1 egg white
Confectioners' sugar, for dusting

1 Put the milk, vanilla bean, and granulated sugar in a medium saucepan and bring just to a simmer over a low heat, then set aside to cool.

2 Scrape the vanilla seeds out of the bean with the point of a sharp knife, and add to the milk. Discard the bean. Melt the butter in a small saucepan and stir in the flour. Cook for 1 minute. Remove from the heat and gradually whisk in the milk. Return the pan to the heat and bring to a boil, stirring all the time.

3 Cook for 1 minute, then remove from the heat and cover the surface of the sauce with plastic wrap. Set aside to cool slightly.

4 Preheat the oven to 375°F. Liberally grease six 6-ounce soufflé dishes and sprinkle the insides with sugar. Whisk the egg yolks into the cooled sauce until smooth. Whisk the egg whites in a clean, grease-free bowl until stiff peaks form. Spoon half into the sauce and stir in gently. Carefully fold in the remaining egg whites with a metal spoon.

5 Pour into the dishes. Bake in the oven for 20–25 minutes, or until well risen, and lightly set. Dust with confectioners' sugar before serving.

Black Cherry &

Chocolate Cake

Makes 10–12 slices

Butter, for greasing
Two 14-ounce cans pitted black
   cherries, drained
½ cup rum
6 eggs
1 cup sugar
1 cup, plus 2 tablespoons self-rising
   flour
5 tablespoons cocoa powder
2½ cups heavy or whipping cream
3 tablespoons black cherry jam
4 ounces semisweet chocolate, grated
8 dark red glacé cherries, to decorate

1 Preheat the oven to 400°F. Grease and base-line two 9-inch springform pans. Put the cherries in a large bowl and pour over half of the rum. Set aside.

2 Put the eggs and sugar, less 3 tablespoons, in a large heatproof bowl set over a saucepan of simmering water. Using a hand-held electric mixer, whisk for 15–20 minutes, or until the mixture is pale, creamy and thick enough to leave a trail.

Remove from the heat. Sift the flour and cocoa powder over the whisked egg mixture and fold in gently but thoroughly.

3 Pour the mixture into the prepared pans, dividing it evenly. Bake in the oven for 12–15 minutes, or until just firm to the touch. Turn out on to a wire rack and let cool.

4 Whip the cream in a bowl until soft peaks form. Whisk in the remaining rum and the 3 tablespoons of sugar. Brush each of the cake layers with the rum that the cherries have been soaking in, then spread the jam evenly over one of the cakes. Top this cake with one-third of the cream and the cherries. Place the other cake on top, then cover the top of the cake with cream, reserving some for the decoration.

5 Sprinkle the top of the cake with the grated chocolate, then pipe 8 rosettes of cream around the top edge of the cake. Top with the glacé cherries. Chill for 45 minutes before serving.

Cherry Cinnamon Cobbler

Serves 4–6

2¼ pounds stoned black cherries
   in heavy syrup
½ cup dried cherries
½ cup packed light brown sugar
2 tablespoons cornstarch
2 tablespoons cold water

For the topping
1½ cups all-purpose flour
Pinch of salt
2 teaspoons baking powder
1 teaspoon ground cinnamon
½ cup packed brown sugar
¾ stick (6 tablespoons) butter, melted
½ cup milk

1 Put a baking sheet in the oven and preheat to 375°F. Drain the cherries, reserving the syrup. Put them with the dried cherries in a large pie dish. Pour 2½ cups of the syrup in a saucepan and add the brown sugar. Slowly bring to a boil, stirring continuously until the sugar has dissolved.

2 Mix the cornstarch and cold water together in a small bowl and stir into the syrup. Cook for 1–2 minutes, or until the syrup thickens. Pour the syrup over the cherries.

3 For the topping, combine the flour, salt, baking powder, cinnamon, and sugar in a bowl. Stir in the melted butter and milk and mix well. Spoon dollops of the mixture over the cherries.

4 Bake for 35–40 minutes, or until the topping is risen and golden.

Tip
A cobbler is fruit topped with a crust, which can be made from cookie dough, pie pastry, or cookie topping, and baked.

Grape Pie

Serves 6

1⅓ cups all-purpose flour, plus extra
  for dusting
Pinch of salt
¼ teaspoon ground ginger
¾ stick (6 tablespoons) cold butter, or
  half butter/half shortening
2 tablespoons cold water
1 tablespoon milk, for glazing
1 tablespoon raw sugar, for sprinkling
Light cream, to serve

For the filling

1½ pounds green or red seedless
  grapes
¼ cup raw sugar, or to taste
2 tablespoons cornstarch
3 tablespoons grape, apple or
  orange juice
1 tablespoon butter

1 Sift the flour, salt and ginger into a mixing bowl. Add the fat and rub it in until the mixture resembles fine bread crumbs. Sprinkle over the water and mix to a firm dough. Knead briefly, then wrap in plastic wrap and chill for 30 minutes. Meanwhile, preheat the oven to 400°F.

2 For the filling, halve the grapes, if large, and put them in a bowl with the sugar. Blend the cornstarch with the fruit juice and pour over the grapes, then toss the mixture gently with your hands to ensure all the fruit is coated.

3 Using an inverted 1-quart baking dish with a rim as a guide, roll out the dough on a floured surface until it is 2 inches larger all around than the dish. Cut off a 1-inch strip from around the edge. Moisten the rim of the dish and position the strip on the rim. Brush with water.

4 Stir the grape mixture, and then tip into the pie dish, piling up the grapes in the center so that the filling is slightly rounded. Dot the top of the fruit with butter. Place the dough lid on top, pressing the edges together to seal. Trim off the excess dough and snip a hole in the top of the pie to allow steam to escape.

5 Crimp the dough edge. Brush with milk, then sprinkle with raw sugar. Bake the pie for 15 minutes, then reduce the temperature to 350°F and bake for a further 20–30 minutes, or until the crust is golden. Serve hot or warm with cream.

Deep-Dish Apple Pie à la Mode

Serves 4–6

1⅔ cups all-purpose flour, plus extra
   for dusting
½ teaspoon salt
1 stick (8 tablespoons) cold butter
¼ cup ice water
Whisked egg white or cream, for glazing
Granulated sugar, for sprinkling
   (optional)
Ice cream, to serve

For the filling
1½ pounds peeled and cored tart
   apples, thinly sliced
1 tablespoon lemon juice
¾ cup granulated sugar
¼ cup packed brown sugar
2 tablespoons all-purpose flour
⅛ teaspoon salt
¼ teaspoon freshly grated nutmeg
¼ teaspoon ground cinnamon
1 tablespoon butter

1 Preheat the oven to 450°F. For the dough, sift the flour and salt into a mixing bowl. Add the butter and rub it in until you get fine bread crumbs. Slowly mix in the water with a fork until the dough forms a ball. Wrap in plastic wrap and chill for 1 hour.

2 Divide the dough into 2 equal-sized balls. Dust the work surface and rolling pin lightly with flour. Flatten each ball of dough, sprinkle the surface with flour, roll from the center into a round about 12 inches in diameter. Place the first round in the base of a 10-inch deep-dish pie pan and gently press the dough into the sides of the pan.

3 Toss the apple slices in lemon juice to prevent them turning brown and arrange them closely together on top of the round of dough. Mix the two kinds of sugar, the flour, salt, nutmeg, cinnamon, and butter in another bowl and sprinkle over the apples.

4 Lay the second round of dough loosely over the apples and fold the overhang under the edges of the dish to seal. Trim off the excess dough. Press firmly around the rim with the tines of a fork. Brush the surface with whisked egg white or cream. For a glistening top, sprinkle lightly with sugar.

5 Bake for 10 minutes on the lowest shelf in the oven, then reduce the temperature to 350°F and bake for a further 30–45 minutes. The apples are done when juice bubbles from the steam vents and the fruit feels tender when skewered. Transfer the pie to a wire rack and let cool for 3 hours. Serve warm with ice cream.

Banoffee Pie

Serves 6–8

1¼ cups all-purpose flour
1 stick (8 tablespoons) cold butter, diced
¼ cup granulated sugar

For the filling
1 stick (8 tablespoons) butter
½ cup light brown sugar
2 tablespoons light corn syrup
14-ounce can sweetened
   condensed skimmed milk
2 medium bananas
1 tablespoon lemon juice
⅔ cup heavy cream
3 ounces semisweet chocolate,
   coarsely grated, to decorate

Tip

If you're not going
to eat the pie within the next
24 hours, place the bananas
before the toffee. This will stop
the banana going brown.
Cover with cream just
before serving.

1 Sift the flour into a bowl. Add the butter and rub it in until the mixture resembles coarse bread crumbs. Stir in the sugar, then mix to a soft dough. Wrap in plastic wrap and chill for 30 minutes.

2 Put a baking sheet in the oven and preheat to 325°F. Press the dough into an 8-inch loose-bottomed tart pan. Prick the base with a fork, then chill for 10 minutes. Line the tart shell with parchment paper and fill with baking beans. Bake blind for 15 minutes. Remove the paper and beans and cook for 10 minutes until the crust is golden and crisp. Transfer to a wire rack to cool.

3 For the filling, put the butter in a saucepan over a low heat. When it starts to melt, add the sugar, corn syrup, and condensed milk. Heat gently until the sugar has dissolved.

4 Bring to a boil, then simmer for 8–10 minutes, stirring until it turns a light caramel color. Cool for a few minutes, then pour into the tart shell and let cool completely.

5 Slice the bananas diagonally. Toss the slices in lemon juice, then arrange in concentric circles in the center of the pie. Whip the cream until soft peaks form, then pipe swirls around the edge. Decorate with grated chocolate.

Two-Crust Prune Pie

Serves 6–8

1¾ cups all-purpose flour
Pinch of salt
½ teaspoon ground cinnamon
1 stick (8 tablespoons) cold butter, or
    half butter/half shortening, diced
3–4 tablespoons cold water
1 tablespoon milk, for glazing
1 tablespoon granulated sugar
Light cream, to serve

For the filling

1 pound whole prunes
1 tablespoon all-purpose flour
¼ cup granulated sugar
2 teaspoons lemon juice
2 teaspoons butter

1 For the filling, put the prunes in a large bowl and pour over enough near-boiling water to just cover them. Let soak for 2 hours.

2 For the pastry, sift the flour, salt, and cinnamon into a mixing bowl. Add the butter and rub it in until the mixture resembles fine bread crumbs. Sprinkle 3 tablespoons water over the surface and mix to a firm dough. Knead briefly, then wrap in plastic wrap and chill for 30 minutes.

3 Drain the prunes, reserving 1 cup of the soaking liquid. Halve the prunes and pit them. Blend the flour, sugar, lemon juice, and a little of the soaking liquid to a paste in a saucepan. Stir in the remaining soaking liquid, then add the prunes and butter. Bring to a boil and simmer for 1–2 minutes, or until thickened, stirring continuously. Remove from the heat and cool.

4 Put a baking sheet in the oven and preheat to 375°F. Roll out two-thirds of the dough on a lightly floured surface to a round about 1½ inches larger than a shallow 8–9-inch pie pan. Ease the dough into the pie pan; leave an overhang of dough.

5 Spoon the prune mixture into the pie shell, then dampen the pastry edge with water. Roll out the remaining dough to make a lid and use to cover the pie, pressing the edges together well to seal. Trim the excess dough with a knife.

6 Crimp the edge of the pie, then decorate by cutting leaves from the dough trimmings. Brush the pie with milk and sprinkle with sugar. Slash the top twice, or make small holes with a skewer to allow steam to escape. Bake for 35–40 minutes, or until the crust is golden brown and crisp. Serve hot with cream.

Peach Cobbler

Serves 4–6

2¼ pounds ripe, but still firm, peaches
    or nectarines (or canned equivalent)
1 tablespoon cornstarch
½ cup, plus 1 tablespoon granulated
    sugar
¼ teaspoon ground cinnamon
Juice of 1 lemon
¼ stick (2 tablespoons) butter, diced
Cream, to serve

For the topping
1¾ cups self-rising flour, plus extra
    for dusting
Pinch of salt
1 teaspoon baking powder
3 tablespoons butter, diced
⅔ cup milk
Beaten egg, for glazing
1 tablespoon confectioners' sugar,
    for dusting

1 Preheat the oven to 325°F. For the filling, drop a few peaches at a time into a saucepan of boiling water, leave for 30–40 seconds, then transfer to a bowl of cold water. Peel and slice the fruit, and pit them.

2 Put the fruit slices in a bowl. Blend the cornstarch, sugar, and cinnamon together, and sprinkle over. Gently toss together with the lemon juice, then transfer to a 9-inch pie pan. Dot the top with butter. Cover with foil, then bake for 20 minutes.

3 For the pastry, sift the flour, salt and baking powder together into a mixing bowl. Add the butter and rub it in until the mixture resembles bread crumbs. Stir in enough milk to give a fairly soft dough.

4 Remove the peaches from the oven and stir. Increase the temperature to 425°F. Roll out the dough on a lightly floured surface until slightly larger than the pie dish. Lightly brush the edges of the dish with water, then put the lid over the filling. Brush the top with beaten egg and make 2 small slits in the top. Bake for 12–15 minutes, or until the top is well risen and golden brown. Dust with confectioners' sugar and serve hot with cream.

Cranberry Pie

Serves 6

1¾ cups all-purpose flour, plus extra
   for dusting
Pinch of salt
1 stick (8 tablespoons) cold butter
2 tablespoons granulated sugar, plus
   extra for topping
1 egg yolk
1–2 tablespoons milk
Whipped cream, to serve

For the filling
1¼ cups granulated sugar
Finely grated zest and juice of
   1 orange
Two 12-ounce bags fresh cranberries

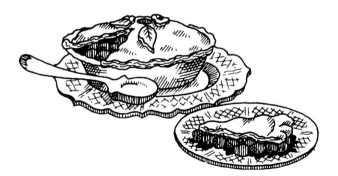

1 Preheat the oven to 400°F. Mix the flour and salt together in a bowl. Add the butter and rub it in until the mixture resembles bread crumbs. Stir in the sugar, then add enough of the egg to make a dough. Wrap in plastic wrap and leave to rest in a cool place for 30 minutes.

2 For the filling, mix the sugar, grated orange zest, and juice together in a bowl. Mix well, then stir in the cranberries. Spoon into a deep 6-cup pie dish.

3 Roll out the dough on a lightly floured surface to fit the top of the dish, adding an extra inch all around. Cut off a 1-inch strip from around the edge. Dampen the rim of the pie dish lightly with water and stick the dough strip in place. Add the milk to any remaining egg yolk, and brush a little of this on to the dough strip. Put the dough lid on top, seal and crimp the edges.

4 Decorate the top of the pie with pastry shapes, if liked. Snip one or two holes in the top of the pie to allow the steam to escape, then brush the pastry with the remaining egg and milk mixture. Sprinkle with sugar. Bake the pie above the center of the oven for 25–35 minutes, or until the crust is golden and crisp. Sprinkle with more sugar and serve with whipped cream.

Key Lime Pie

Serves 6–8

⅔ stick (5 tablespoons) butter, melted,
   plus extra for greasing
35 vanilla wafers
2–3 tablespoons granulated sugar

For the filling
7-ounce can sweetened condensed
   milk
½ cup freshly squeezed lime juice
3 egg yolks

To decorate (optional)
1 cup heavy cream, whipped
Zest of 1 lime

1 Lightly grease a 9-inch pie pan. Put the wafers in a strong plastic bag and crush with a rolling pin until very fine crumbs form. Alternatively, use a food processor. Put the crumbs into a large bowl, add the sugar and butter and mix well.

2 Pour the crumbs into the prepared pie pan and, using the back of the spoon, press the crumbs evenly onto the base and side of the pan. Chill while you make the filling.

3 For the filling, whisk the condensed milk, lime juice, and egg yolks together in a bowl until well blended and thickened. Pour into the pie shell and chill until set. Decorate with a little whipped cream and lime zest, if liked. Serve with additional whipped cream.

Tip
This is best served
very cold, so place it
in the freezer for
15–20 minutes
before serving.

Blackberry & Apple Pie

Serves 6–8

3 cups all-purpose flour, plus extra for
dusting
⅓ cup confectioners' sugar
1 stick (8 tablespoons) butter
1 egg, plus 1 egg yolk
Milk, for glazing
Granulated sugar, for sprinkling

For the filling
3 small tart apples, peeled, cored
and thinly sliced
5½ cups blackberries
1 cup granulated sugar
1 tablespoon cornstarch
½ teaspoon ground allspice
½ teaspoon freshly grated nutmeg

1 Sift the flour and confectioners' sugar into a mixing bowl. Add the butter and rub it in until the mixture resembles bread crumbs. Add the egg and egg yolk, and mix quickly to a rough dough. Wrap in plastic wrap and let rest in a cool place, not the refrigerator, for 20 minutes.

2 Put a baking sheet in the oven and preheat to 400°F. Put the apple slices in a bowl, add the blackberries, sugar, cornstarch, allspice, and nutmeg and toss gently to mix.

3 Roll out just less than half the dough on a lightly floured surface and use to line a 10-inch pie pan. Spoon the filling on top.

4 Roll out the remaining dough to a round 1-inch wider than the rim of the dish. Moisten the rim of the dough with water, then place the dough on top. Seal and trim off the excess dough. Crimp the edges and snip a hole in the top to allow steam to escape. Brush the pie with milk and sprinkle with sugar.

5 Bake for 15 minutes, then reduce the oven temperature to 350°F and bake for a further 20–25 minutes. Serve warm.

Cherry Strudel

Serves 8

4 large sheets phyllo pastry, thawed if
frozen
$\frac{1}{3}$ stick (3 tablespoons) unsalted butter,
melted
Confectioners' sugar, for dusting

For the filling
1¼ pounds fresh sweet cherries,
pitted and halved
3 tablespoons ground almonds
6 tablespoons granulated sugar
½ cup fresh cake crumbs

1 Preheat the oven to 375°F. For the filling, put the cherries, ground almonds, granulated sugar, and cake crumbs in a bowl and stir to combine.

2 Cover the phyllo pastry with a slightly damp kitchen towel to prevent it drying out. Lay a sheet of the pastry on a large, flat baking sheet and brush with a little melted butter. Lay a second phyllo sheet over the top and brush with butter. Repeat this twice more so that you have a rectangle of 4 sheets of phyllo.

3 Spoon the cherry mixture over the top, leaving a gap of 2 inches around the edge. Roll up the longest side—like you would a jelly roll. Tuck in the ends and form into a horseshoe shape.

4 Brush the surface of the pastry with more butter and bake for 25 minutes. Dust with confectioners' sugar and serve warm or at room temperature.

Linzertorte with a Lattice Top

Serves 8

1¾ cups all-purpose flour, plus extra
    for dusting
Pinch of salt
¼ cup ground almonds
1¼ sticks (10 tablespoons) cold
    unsalted butter, diced
¼ cup packed light brown sugar
2 eggs, separated
3–4 teaspoons cold water
Confectioners' sugar, for dusting
Heavy cream, to serve

For the filling
3½ cups fresh raspberries
½ cup granulated sugar
2 teaspoons cornstarch mixed
    with 2 teaspoons cold water
1 tablespoon fresh lemon juice

1 Mix the flour, salt, and ground almonds in a mixing bowl. Add the butter and rub it in until the mixture resembles fine bread crumbs. Stir in the brown sugar. Mix the egg yolks with the cold water. Add to the dough and bring the dough together. Knead briefly until smooth. Wrap in plastic wrap and chill for 30 minutes.

2 Put the raspberries and sugar into a saucepan over a low heat. Bring to a boil, stir in the cornstarch mixture and cook for 2 minutes. Remove from the heat, stir in the lemon juice and leave until cold.

3 Put a baking sheet in the oven and preheat to 400°F. Roll out two-thirds of the dough on a lightly floured surface. Roll the dough into a round at least 2 inches larger than a deep, loose-bottomed 8-inch fluted tart pan. Gently roll the dough onto the rolling pin, then unroll it over the pan to cover. Carefully press the dough into the edge of the pan, removing any overhanging dough. Prick the base all over with a fork. Chill for 20 minutes.

4 Roll the dough trimmings with the remaining dough. Cut into 10 long strips, each 1 inch wide using a zigzag cutter. Spoon the raspberry mixture into the prepared shell. Dampen the edges of the dough using the egg white, then lay the strips over the top of the filling to make a lattice pattern. Gently press the edges of the dough together, and trim off the excess.

5 Bake for 35–40 minutes until the crust is golden. Let cool for 5 minutes. Remove from the pan and let stand for 10–15 minutes. Dust with confectioners' sugar and serve warm with cream.

Hot Waffles & Banana
with Toffee Brandy Sauce

Serves 2

2 frozen waffles
2 scoops vanilla ice cream
2 bananas, sliced

For the sauce
¼ cup heavy cream
2 tablespoons dark brown sugar
3 tablespoons butter
2 tablespoons brandy

1 For the sauce, put the cream, sugar, butter, and brandy in a small saucepan and heat gently until the sugar has dissolved. Increase the heat and simmer for 3 minutes, or until thickened.

2 Warm the waffles in the microwave, or heat in the oven or toaster according to the instructions on the packet. Put a generous scoop of ice cream and half the sliced bananas on each one. Drizzle over the sauce and serve.

Jelly Roll
with Lemon Cream

Serves 6

4 large eggs
½ cup granulated sugar, plus extra
    for dusting
¾ cup all-purpose flour
Sifted confectioners' sugar and finely
    grated lemon zest, to decorate

For the filling
8 ounces mascarpone cheese
Finely grated zest and juice of ½ lemon
2 tablespoons freshly squeezed
    orange juice
¼ cup confectioners' sugar

1 Preheat the oven to 425°F. Grease a 10 x 13-inch baking sheet with side. Line with parchment paper.

2 For the cake, using a hand-held electric mixer, whisk the eggs and sugar together in a large bowl until the mixture is pale, creamy, and thick enough to leave a trail on the surface when the beaters are lifted.

3 Sift and fold in the flour in three batches. Pour the mixture into the prepared pan, tilting the pan backwards and forwards to spread evenly. Bake in the oven for about 10 minutes, or until risen and golden and the cake springs back when lightly pressed.

4 While the cake is baking, lay a sheet of parchment paper on a work surface and sprinkle liberally with granulated sugar.

5 Quickly turn the hot cake out onto the sugar-dusted paper and remove the lining paper. Trim off the crusty edges, score a cut a ½ inch in from one of the shorter ends, then roll up the cake from the scored short end with the paper inside. Place on a wire rack and let cool.

6 For the filling, put all the filling ingredients in a bowl and beat together until smooth and well mixed. Carefully unroll the cake, remove the paper and spread the filling mixture evenly over the cake. Re-roll the cake. To decorate, sprinkle the cake with sifted confectioners' sugar and lemon zest. Serve in slices.

Crumb Pie

Serves 6

1 cup all-purpose flour, plus extra
   for dusting
Pinch of salt
$\frac{1}{3}$ stick (3 tablespoons) cold butter,
   diced
1 egg yolk
1½ tablespoons cold water

For the topping
$\frac{1}{3}$ cup all-purpose flour
$\frac{3}{4}$ cup cake crumbs
1 teaspoon ground cinnamon
Pinch of freshly grated nutmeg
Pinch of ground ginger
$\frac{2}{3}$ stick (5 tablespoons) butter

For the filling
$\frac{3}{4}$ cup packed light brown sugar
$\frac{1}{3}$ cup hot water
2 eggs, lightly beaten
½ cup raisins

1 Sift the flour and salt into a mixing bowl. Add the butter and rub it in until the mixture resembles bread crumbs. Mix the egg yolk and water together in another bowl. Add all but 2 teaspoons of the egg mixture and mix to a firm dough. Knead until smooth, wrap in plastic wrap, and chill for 30 minutes.

2 Preheat the oven to 400°F. Roll out the pastry on a lightly floured surface and use to line an 8-inch tart pan. Prick the base all over, then chill for 15 minutes. Line the tart shell with parchment paper and fill with baking beans. Bake for 15 minutes. Remove the paper and beans, brush the base with the reserved egg and bake for a further 5 minutes. Reduce the oven temperature to 325°F.

3 For the topping, sift the flour into a bowl and stir in the cake crumbs and spices. Add the butter and rub it in until the mixture resembles coarse bread crumbs. Set aside.

4 For the filling, put the sugar, hot water, and eggs into a bowl set over a saucepan of simmering water, stirring for 7–8 minutes until the mixture thickens. Spread out the raisins in the tart shell, then pour in the filling. Sprinkle over the crumb mixture and bake for 20–25 minutes, or until lightly set.

Baked Apples with

Walnut Jackets

Makes 14

1 cup walnuts
4 ginger cookies, broken
⅔ cup light brown sugar
1 teaspoon ground cinnamon
½ teaspoon Chinese five spice powder
4 large cooking apples
⅓ stick (3 tablespoons) butter, melted
Plain yogurt, to serve

1 Preheat the oven to 350°F. Blend the walnuts, ginger cookies, brown sugar, cinnamon, and five spice powder in a food processor until the mixture forms fine crumbs.

2 Core the apples, then score the skin on each one around the circumference, two-thirds of the way down the fruit. Peel off all the skin above the mark. Take a thin slice off the bottom of each apple, if necessary, so that they stand straight.

3 Put the apples in a baking dish and fill each one with the walnut mixture, packing it down firmly. Brush the exposed flesh on the top of each apple with the butter and press the remaining walnut mixture onto it so that each apple is topped with a walnut jacket. Drizzle any remaining butter over, being careful not to dislodge the crust.

4 Bake the apples for 45 minutes or until tender. Serve hot or cold with natural yogurt.

Banana & Toffee

Cheesecake

Serves 10–12

1¾ cup all-purpose flour, plus extra for
dusting
Pinch of salt
1 stick (8 tablespoons) butter, diced
¼ cup granulated sugar
3–4 tablespoons cold water

For the filling
4 ounces semisweet chocolate, melted,
plus extra to decorate
3 large ripe but firm bananas,
thickly sliced
Juice of ½ lemon
8 ounces mascarpone cheese
⅔ cup heavy cream, lightly whipped
15-ounce jar thick toffee or caramel
sauce/spread

1 Sift the flour and salt into a mixing bowl. Add the butter and rub it in until the mixture resembles coarse bread crumbs. Stir in the sugar. Add 3 tablespoons cold water and mix to a dough. Knead briefly until the dough is smooth. Shape into a ball, wrap in plastic wrap and chill for 20 minutes.

2 Roll out the dough on a lightly floured surface to form a round at least 2 inches larger than a 9-inch plain pastry ring set on a baking sheet. Use the pastry round to line the ring, pressing the edges and trimming the overhanging dough. Prick the base with a fork. Chill for 20 minutes.

3 Preheat the oven to 400°F. Line the pastry shell with parchment paper and fill with baking beans and bake in the oven for 12 minutes. Remove the paper and beans and bake for a further 10-12 minutes, or until golden. Remove from the oven and let cool. Using a pastry brush, paint the inside of the pastry shell with melted chocolate. Chill until set.

4 For the cheesecake, toss the bananas in the lemon juice and set aside. Beat the mascarpone cheese in a bowl until softened, then stir in the whipped cream. Carefully fold the cream mixture and most of the caramel sauce together (reserving a little sauce for decoration), leaving them marbled. Spoon the mixture into the pastry shell, then scatter the banana over the top. Drizzle the remaining caramel over the bananas. Chill before serving.

CHOCOLATE HEAVEN

- Mississippi Mud Pie
- Chocolate Cream Pie
- Chocolate Espresso Pots
- Chocolate Brioche Pudding
- Chocolate Raspberry Torte
- Chocolate & Orange Mousse
- White & Dark Chocolate Cheesecake with Raspberries
- Chocolate & Chestnut Meringue Torte
- Marshmallow & Chocolate Ice Cream
- Rich Mocha Pots
- Bitter Chocolate Sorbet
- Rich Chocolate Tartlets
- Chocolate Marquise with Vanilla Crème Anglaise
- Chocolate Fudge Cake
- Marshmallow & Chocolate Pie

- Chocolate Doughnuts
- White Chocolate Parfait
- Kahlua & Chocolate Trifle
- Chocolate Crêpes with Caramelized Bananas & Cream
- Chocolate & Toffee Tart
- Chocolate Tiramisù
- Cappuccino Truffle Cake
- Chocolate Amaretto Cheesecake
- Chocolate Pudding
- Peppermint Chocolate Layer Cake
- Double Chocolate Chunky Brownies
- Super-quick Bailey's Chocolate Mousse
- Chocolate & Brandy Truffles
- Chocolate Layer Cake

CHAPTER TWO

CHOCOLATE HEAVEN

Mississippi Mud Pie

Serves 6–8

²/₃ stick (5 tablespoons) butter, softened
1 cup, plus 1 tablespoon all-purpose
　flour
2 tablespoons cold water
½ cup chopped walnuts
²/₃ cup confectioners' sugar
8-ounce tub cream cheese, softened
2 cups heavy cream, whipped
6-ounce package instant chocolate
　pudding mix
4 cups milk
1 heaping teaspoon cocoa powder

To decorate
Sifted cocoa powder
Chopped nuts

1 Preheat the oven to 350°F. Put the butter and flour in a mixing bowl and rub together lightly until the mixture resembles fine bread crumbs. Stir in the water. Distribute the walnuts through the mixture, then press the mixture into a 9-inch pie pan. Bake for 12–15 minutes. Remove from the oven and let cool.

2 Combine the confectioners' sugar, cream cheese, and half of the whipped cream, reserving the rest for the topping in another bowl. Gently spread the mixture over the first cooked layer. Chill while you prepare the pudding mix with the milk, according to the instructions on the package, in a separate bowl. Mix in the cocoa powder. Remove the chilled pie from the refrigerator and spread the chocolate pudding mix over the second layer. Top with the reserved whipped cream, dust with a fine layer of cocoa powder and sprinkle with chopped nuts. Chill for a further 4 hours before serving.

Chocolate Cream Pie

Serves 6–8

1⅓ cups all-purpose flour
2 tablespoons granulated sugar
1 stick (8 tablespoons) butter, diced
1 egg yolk
2–3 teaspoons cold water
Chocolate curls, to decorate

For the filling
⅓ cup cornstarch
½ cup granulated sugar
⅔ cup light cream
1¼ cups milk
3 ounces semisweet chocolate, in pieces
2 egg yolks
2 tablespoons butter

For the topping
1 cup heavy cream
½ teaspoon pure vanilla extract
2 teaspoons confectioners' sugar, sifted

1 Sift the flour and sugar into a mixing bowl. Add the butter and rub it in until the mixture resembles fine bread crumbs. Mix the egg yolk and 2 teaspoons water together and sprinkle over the dry ingredients. Mix to a dough, adding extra water if needed. Knead, cover and chill for 30 minutes.

2 Put a baking sheet in the oven and preheat to 400°F. Roll out the pastry on a lightly floured surface and use to line a shallow 8-9 inch pie pan. Chill for 10 minutes. Line the pie shell with parchment paper and fill with baking beans. Bake blind for 15 minutes. Remove the paper and beans and bake for 8-10 minutes until golden and crisp. Cool on a wire rack.

3 Mix the cornstarch and sugar together in a non-stick saucepan. Gradually blend in the cream, then stir in the milk and chocolate. Gently heat, stirring, until the chocolate melts and the mixture thickens and boils. Remove from the heat.

4 Beat the egg yolks. Stir in a few spoonfuls of the chocolate mixture, then pour and stir the egg mixture back into the chocolate mixture in the pan. Continue to stir for 1 minute, but do not boil. Remove from the heat and stir in the butter. Cool slightly, then pour into the pie shell. Press a circle of dampened parchment paper on top. Cool, then chill for 2 hours. Remove the paper.

5 For the topping, pour the cream into a chilled bowl. Stir in the vanilla and sugar. Whip until soft peaks form, then spoon into a piping bag with a large star nozzle and pipe a lattice pattern on top. Scatter with chocolate curls and serve.

Chocolate Espresso Pots

Serves 8

6 ounces semisweet chocolate, 70 per cent cocoa solids, broken into pieces, plus a little extra to decorate

1⅓ cups strong, fresh espresso coffee

2 tablespoons coffee liqueur or whiskey

¼ cup granulated sugar

6 egg yolks

¼ cup heavy cream, to serve

1 Put the chocolate into a heatproof bowl along with the coffee and coffee liqueur or whiskey. Set the bowl over a saucepan of simmering water. The bowl should not touch the water. Leave, without stirring, until the chocolate has melted, then stir until smooth. Remove from the heat and stir in the sugar. Let cool for about 5 minutes.

2 Beat in the egg yolks, then pour the mixture through a sieve into 8 small espresso cups or ramekins. Let cool, then chill for at least 4 hours, or overnight.

3 When ready to serve, lightly whip the cream and put a spoonful on top of each chocolate cup. Sprinkle over a little extra grated chocolate and serve.

Tip

Chocolate should always be heated in a heatproof bowl set over a saucepan of simmering water so that the heat doesn't burn the chocolate. Put half of the chocolate in a heatproof bowl, and stir with a spatula when the outside edges of the chocolate begin to melt. Gradually add the rest of the chocolate. When it has almost melted remove the bowl from the heat, and continue stirring until the chocolate is smooth and shiny.

Chocolate Brioche Pudding

Serves 8

1 pound brioche loaf

⅔ stick (5 tablespoons) unsalted butter, softened

½ ounce semisweet chocolate

1⅓ cups whipping cream

2 cups prepared custard (see p.131)

1 cup milk

1 Using a serrated bread knife, cut the crusts off the brioche loaf, then cut into ½ inch thick slices. Grease a 9-inch square gratin dish with a little of the butter then sparingly spread the remaining butter over the brioche. Lay half the slices over the base of the dish.

2 Put half the chocolate on a board and roughly chop with a large sharp knife. Sprinkle evenly over the brioche, then top with the remaining buttered slices. Finely chop the remaining chocolate. Bring the cream to a boil in a small saucepan, add the chocolate and stir until melted.

3 Whisk the custard and milk together and stir in the chocolate cream. Pour over the brioche and let soak for 30 minutes. Preheat the oven to 300°F. Put the dish in a roasting pan and pour enough hot water to come halfway up the side of the dish. Cook in the oven for about 55 minutes. It should be firm with a little wobble. Let pudding stand for 5 minutes before serving.

Chocolate Raspberry Torte

Serves 6–8

¼ **stick (2½ tablespoons) unsalted**
   butter, plus extra for greasing
⅓ **cup all-purpose flour**
¼ **cup cocoa powder, plus extra for**
   dusting
3 **large eggs**
⅓ **cup granulated sugar**
¼ **cup cream**
¼ **cup orange liqueur**
1⅓ **cups fresh or frozen raspberries**
1 **tablespoon confectioners' sugar**
2½ **ounces semisweet chocolate, grated**

1 Grease and line a 9-inch round cake pan. Preheat the oven to 350°F. Sift the flour and cocoa together and melt the butter. Break the eggs into a bowl and add the granulated sugar. Put the bowl over a saucepan of hot water and whisk with an electric hand-held whisk until pale and the yolk falls from the whisk in a thick ribbon.

2 Sift the flour and cocoa in 3 batches over the eggs and gently fold in, drizzling a little butter around the bowl in between each batch. Discard any white sediment at the base of the pan.

3 Pour into the prepared pan and bake for 20 minutes until brown and the top springs back when pressed lightly. Let cool in the pan for 2–3 minutes, then turn out on to a wire rack to cool completely.

4 For the filling, whip the cream and liqueur until the mixture forms soft peaks. Fold in the raspberries, sugar, and chocolate.

5 Cut the cake through horizontally to make two layers. Line an 8-inch springform pan with parchment paper and trim the cake to fit the base of the pan. Put one of the cake halves at the bottom. Pile in the raspberry cream and top with the remaining cake. Press down evenly and freeze for 4 hours until the filling is firm. Dust the top with cocoa then remove from the pan and serve in slices.

Tip
To cut the torte
into clean wedges,
wipe the knife
between slices.

Chocolate & Orange Mousse

Serves 4

8 ounces good-quality semisweet
   chocolate, broken into pieces
Grated zest and juice of 1 large orange
1 tablespoon Grand Marnier
4 eggs, separated
⅓ cup confectioners' sugar
⅔ cup heavy cream
Pared strips of orange zest, to decorate
   (optional)

1 Put the chocolate in a heatproof bowl. Add the orange zest and juice and the Grand Marnier and set over a saucepan of simmering water. Heat until the chocolate has melted, then stir until smooth. Let cool.

2 Whisk the egg yolks and confectioners' sugar together until the mixture becomes pale and frothy. Stir into the cooled chocolate mixture.

3 Lightly whip the cream and fold into the mousse mixture. Whisk the egg whites in a clean, grease-free bowl until soft peaks form and carefully fold into the mixture. Pour into 4 custard cups, individual ramekins, a soufflé dish, or a glass bowl and chill for 3–4 hours until set. Decorate with orange zest, if liked.

White & Dark Chocolate

Cheesecake with Raspberries

Serves 2

½ cup graham cracker crumbs

⅓ stick (3 tablespoons) unsalted butter, melted

1 tablespoon cocoa powder

For the filling

2½ ounces white chocolate

2½ ounces cream cheese

6 tablespoons crème fraîche or sour cream

2 tablespoons confectioners' sugar

To decorate

½ cup raspberries

1 ounce semisweet chocolate curls or grated semisweet chocolate

1 tablespoon cocoa powder, for dusting

1 Mix the graham cracker crumbs, butter and cocoa together in a bowl. Use two 3-inch round cookie cutters to shape the base. Place the cutters on a flat plate and divide the crumb mixture between each of them. Press down on the crumb mixture until firmly packed. Alternatively, you can line the base of two large ramekins with the crumb crust. Put in the refrigerator to chill while you make the filling.

2 Melt the chocolate in a bowl set over a saucepan of simmering water. Beat all the ingredients together for the filling and pour on top of the crusts. Chill for 2 hours, or until firm. Lift off the biscuit cutters, top with raspberries, chocolate curls, or grated chocolate and dust with cocoa.

Chocolate & Chestnut

Meringue Torte

Serves 8–10

5 egg whites

1⅓ cups granulated sugar

2 teaspoons pure vanilla extract

1¾ cups heavy cream

10 ounces semisweet chocolate, broken
into pieces

7½ ounces unsweetened chestnut purée

3 tablespoons brandy

¾ cup confectioners' sugar, sifted

1 tablespoon cocoa powder, sifted,
to decorate

1 Preheat the oven to 250°F. Line 3 baking sheets with parchment paper. Draw a circle around the base of an 8-inch cake pan on each piece of paper.

2 Whisk the egg whites in a clean, grease-free bowl until stiff peaks form. Beat in the sugar a tablespoon at a time—the mixture should be stiff and glossy. Fold in the vanilla extract.

3 Spoon equal quantities of meringue mixture into the middle of each circle and spread out evenly to the edges. Bake for 2 hours, then peel off the paper and let cool on wire racks.

4 Heat the cream in a saucepan until almost boiling. Remove from the heat and add the chocolate, stirring, until it has melted. Set aside to cool, then chill for about 45 minutes, or until the mixture starts to thicken. Using an electric mixer, beat the chocolate mixture for 2–3 minutes until light and airy.

5 Mix the chestnut purée with the brandy and confectioners' sugar. Spread half of the chocolate cream over the base of one meringue disc, then spread half of the chestnut mixture over the chocolate. Put a second meringue disc on top and repeat with the remaining chocolate and chestnut mixture. Top with the remaining meringue and dust with cocoa.

Marshmallow & Chocolate

Ice Cream

Serves 8

8 ounces milk chocolate, broken into
   pieces
6½ ounces mini marshmallows
3 tablespoons water
1¾ cups freshly prepared
   vanilla pudding
1⅓ cups heavy cream

1 Put the chocolate in a heatproof bowl with three-quarters of the marshmallows. Add the water and set the bowl over a saucepan of gently simmering water. Melt the chocolate and stir until smooth, then set aside to cool a little.

2 Stir the cooled chocolate mixture into the vanilla pudding. Fold the remaining marshmallows into the mixture. Lightly whip the cream and fold in. Pour the mixture into a 5-cup terrine or loaf pan and freeze until hard. You may want to line the base of the terrine or pan with nonstick parchment paper to make it easier to unmold.

3 To serve, dip the base of the terrine or pan in hot water and invert on to a serving plate. Cut the ice cream into thick slices.

Rich Mocha Pots

Makes 6–8 pots

6 ounces semisweet chocolate, broken
    into pieces
3 tablespoons strong black coffee
1 tablespoon butter
4 eggs, separated
2 tablespoons brandy
¼ cup confectioners' sugar
Whipped cream
Grated chocolate or curls, to decorate

Tip

To make the chocolate
curls, run a vegetable
peeler along the edge of
a bar of chocolate.

1 Melt the chocolate in a bowl set over a saucepan of hot water. Stir in the coffee and butter until smooth. Remove from the heat and whisk in the egg yolks one by one until the mixture is smooth and glossy. Whisk in the brandy, then set aside to cool and thicken slightly while you are whisking the egg whites.

2 Whisk the egg whites in a clean, grease-free bowl until stiff. Gradually add the sugar and continue whisking until glossy and thick. Fold into the cooled chocolate mixture.

3 Pour into 6 or 8 small teacups or ramekins and chill for 3–4 hours until firm. Top with whipped cream and decorate with grated chocolate or chocolate curls.

Bitter Chocolate Sorbet

Serves 4

8 ounces bitter chocolate

1 cup, plus 2 tablespoons
  granulated sugar

2 tablespoons cocoa powder

2 cups water

Tip

For a smooth product,
process the sorbet mixture
once during freezing and refreeze.
This technique breaks up ice
crystals. Sorbet melts quickly
at room temperature, so
serve quickly.

1 Put the chocolate in a food processor and process until finely chopped. Put the sugar, cocoa, and water in a saucepan and slowly bring to a boil, stirring, to dissolve the sugar. Bring to a boil, then simmer for 5 minutes.

2 Pour the chocolate syrup into the food processor and process until the mixture is completely smooth and the chocolate has melted. Pour into a shallow container and set aside to cool. Once cool, put in the freezer to harden for 2–3 hours. Process until smooth in the food processor. Return to the container and freeze until hard.

Rich Chocolate Tartlets

Makes 6

12 ounces ready-made sweet pie crust
   dough
Flour, for dusting
3½ ounces chocolate
2 eggs
2 tablespoons granulated sugar
⅔ cup heavy cream

Tip
The dough always
needs to rest before
baking to help
prevent shrinkage
during cooking.

1 Preheat the oven to 400°F. Divide the pastry into six pieces. Roll out each piece thinly on a lightly floured surface and use to line six individual tartlet pans. Chill for 20 minutes. Prick the bases and line with parchment paper and baking beans. Bake blind for 15 minutes.

2 Remove the paper and beans and bake for a further 5 minutes. Remove from the oven and set aside. Reduce the oven temperature to 375°F.

3 Melt the chocolate in a bowl set over a saucepan of simmering water. Stir, then set aside to cool slightly. Whisk the eggs and sugar in another bowl until pale. Whisk in the cream, then the melted chocolate. Pour the chocolate mixture into the tartlet shells and bake for 15 minutes until set.

Chocolate Marquise with

Vanilla Crème Anglaise

Serves 6–8

10 ounces bitter chocolate, broken
  into pieces
¼ cup very strong coffee
1 stick (8 tablespoons) butter
9 tablespoons granulated sugar
4 egg yolks
1¾ cups heavy cream

For the vanilla crème anglaise
1⅓ cups milk
1 vanilla bean, split
4 egg yolks
9 tablespoons granulated sugar

1 Line a 8½ x 4½ x 2½ inch loaf pan or terrine dish with plastic wrap. Put the chocolate and coffee in a heatproof bowl set over a saucepan of simmering water and heat until the chocolate has melted. Stir, then set aside to cool.

2 Beat the butter with 5 tablespoons of the sugar until pale and fluffy. Whisk the egg yolks with the remaining 4 tablespoons sugar in another bowl until thickened and pale. Lightly whip the cream in a separate bowl until it just begins to hold its shape.

3 Beat the melted chocolate into the butter and fold in the egg yolk mixture, followed by the cream. Pour into the loaf pan and chill for 5-6 hours.

4 For the crème anglaise, bring the milk just to a boil with the vanilla bean. Beat the egg yolks and sugar together. Add the hot milk, then return the mixture to the pan and stir over a low heat until it starts to thicken. Cool, then scrape out the seeds from the vanilla bean and stir into the cold custard. Chill until ready to serve.

5 To serve, turn the mousse out onto a serving plate and serve with the vanilla crème anglaise.

Chocolate Fudge Cake

Serves 8

1½ sticks (12 tablespoons) unsalted
   butter, plus extra for greasing
8 ounces semisweet chocolate,
   broken into pieces
¼ cup water
¾ cup packed light brown sugar
4 eggs, beaten
1 cup self-rising flour
½ cup ground almonds

For the filling

½ cup cocoa powder
¾ cup packed light brown sugar
⅓ cup confectioners' sugar
1½ sticks (12 tablespoons) unsalted
   butter, melted
¼ cup boiling water

For the icing

4 ounces semisweet chocolate
3 tablespoons unsalted butter
1 ounce milk chocolate, melted
   (optional)

1 Preheat the oven to 350°F. Grease and line two 8-inch cake pans. Melt the chocolate with the water in a bowl set over a saucepan of simmering water. Let cool slightly.

2 Cream the butter and sugar together until light and fluffy. Gradually add the beaten eggs. Stir in the melted chocolate, then fold in the flour and ground almonds. Pour into the prepared cake pans.

3 Bake for 25 minutes. Let cool a little, then turn out both cake halves onto a wire rack. With a long sharp knife, slice them through the middle horizontally so you have four layers.

4 For the filling, mix the cocoa powder, brown sugar, and confectioners' sugar together. Beat in the melted butter and stir in the water to make a smooth paste. Let harden in the refrigerator for about 20 minutes, then spread evenly over three layers of the cake and sandwich together. Set the final cake layer on top.

5 For the icing, melt the chocolate and butter together in a bowl set over a saucepan of simmering water. Beat until glossy then let cool until you have a spreading consistency. Smooth evenly over the top of the cake. Drizzle melted milk chocolate over in zigzag patterns, if liked.

Marshmallow

& Chocolate Pie

Serves 8–10

1⅓ cups graham cracker crumbs

¾ stick (6 tablespoons) unsalted butter, melted

For the filling

Two 8-ounce packages cream cheese

½ cup, plus 2 tablespoons granulated sugar

1 teaspoon pure vanilla extract

3 whole eggs, beaten

2 egg yolks

4 ounces mini marshmallows

For the topping

1⅓ cups heavy cream

5 ounces semisweet chocolate, broken into small pieces

1 Mix the graham cracker crumbs and melted butter together in a bowl, then press into the base of a 9-inch springform cake pan. Chill for 30 minutes, or until firm. Wrap the outside of the pan in foil. Meanwhile, put a baking sheet in the oven and preheat to 350°F.

2 To make the filling, mix the cream cheese, sugar, and vanilla extract together in a bowl. Beat in the eggs and egg yolks, then fold in the marshmallows. Spoon the mixture into the cake pan and level the top.

3 Put the pie in a roasting pan half-full of boiling water and bake for 50 minutes. Let cool, then chill for 2–3 hours, or until firm.

4 For the topping, put the cream in a saucepan and bring to boiling point. Remove from the heat and stir in the chocolate until smooth. Cool for 10 minutes, then pour the sauce over the pie. Chill until the chocolate has set.

Chocolate Doughnuts

Makes 8

1¾ cups all-purpose flour, plus extra
    for dusting
1 envelope fast-action dry yeast
Pinch of salt
¼ cup granulated sugar
¼ stick (2 tablespoons) butter, plus
    extra for greasing
⅔ cup milk
2 egg yolks
Vegetable oil, for deep-frying
1½ ounces milk chocolate, broken into
    pieces

1 Mix the flour, yeast, and salt together in a
mixing bowl. Add the sugar, then add the
butter and rub it in until the mixture resembles
fine bread crumbs.

2 Heat the milk in a saucepan until it is warm,
then whisk in the egg yolks. Add the liquid to
the flour mixture and mix to a soft dough. Cover
with plastic wrap and leave in a warm place for
about 1 hour, or until the dough has doubled in size.

3 Grease a large baking sheet. Punch down the
dough and knead on a well-floured surface for
5–10 minutes. Roll out the dough until ½ inch thick,
and stamp out rounds with a plain biscuit cutter.
Make a hole in the middle of each round with your
finger. Put the doughnuts on the baking sheet and
set aside for 40–60 minutes until doubled in size.

4 Heat the oil in a large, deep saucepan to 375°F
and deep-fry the doughnuts one at a time for
about 5 minutes, or until golden brown. Drain on
paper towels and let cool.

5 Put the milk chocolate in a heatproof bowl
set over a saucepan of simmering water. Heat
until melted, then remove from the heat. Stir, then
let cool lightly. Dip the rounded tops of the doughnuts
in the melted chocolate and set aside to set.

White Chocolate Parfait

Serves 4

6 ounces white chocolate, broken
  into pieces
2 tablespoons milk
1 vanilla bean
4 egg yolks
½ cup confectioners' sugar
1⅓ cups whipping cream

To serve
Rich chocolate sauce
Fresh fruit

Tip
Always cover ice cream when storing in the freezer so it does not absorb flavors from other foods.

1 Melt the chocolate with the milk in a bowl set over a saucepan of gently simmering water. Stir until smooth, then set aside to cool.

2 Split the vanilla bean lengthwise and scrape out the seeds. Mix the seeds with the egg yolks and confectioners' sugar, then beat with an electric whisk until light and fluffy. Stir in the melted chocolate.

3 Lightly whip the cream and fold into the mixture. Divide the mousse among four ramekins or dariole molds and freeze for at least 4 hours until hard.

4 To serve, briefly dip the base of the molds into warm water and turn out on to serving plates. Serve with rich chocolate sauce and fresh fruit.

Kahlua Chocolate Trifle

Serves 4–6

Butter, for greasing
⅔ cup strong fresh coffee
¼ cup Kahlua or other coffee liqueur
6 ounces store-bought ladyfingers
16 ounces mascarpone cheese
⅓ cup granulated sugar
2 teaspoons pure vanilla extract
1⅓ cups heavy cream
3½ ounces semisweet chocolate, grated
Cocoa powder, for dusting

1 Grease and line a 9 x 5-inch loaf pan with plastic wrap. Mix the coffee and liqueur together in a bowl. Dip the ladyfingers into the mixture and use some to line the base of the pan.

2 Put the mascarpone into a large bowl, then beat in the sugar and vanilla extract. Add the cream a little at a time, beating on a slow speed until smooth.

3 Spoon half of the mixture on top of the ladyfingers in the pan and spread over evenly. Add half the grated chocolate, then repeat a layer of the dipped ladyfingers, the remaining creamed mixture, grated chocolate, and a final layer of dipped ladyfingers. Drizzle any remaining coffee mixture over the top.

4 Cover with a layer of plastic wrap, then chill for 2–3 hours. Remove from the pan and peel off the plastic wrap. Dust with a generous amount of cocoa powder, slice, and serve.

Chocolate Crêpes with
Caramelized Bananas & Cream

Makes 10 crêpes

1 cup, plus 2 tablespoons
   all-purpose flour
2 tablespoons cocoa powder
2 tablespoons granulated sugar
2 eggs, beaten
¾ cup, plus 2 tablespoons milk
6 tablespoons water
1 tablespoon sunflower oil, plus extra
   for frying
4 bananas, sliced
⅓ cup confectioners' sugar
1⅓ cups cream, whipped

Tip
Pancakes are ready to flip
when their surface is covered
with bubbles, their edges look
dry and a peek at their undersides
reveals a golden brown color.
Turn them gently, barely
lifting them off
the pan.

1 Mix the flour, cocoa powder, and granulated sugar together in a large bowl. Add the beaten eggs and slowly pour in the milk and water, beating until you have a smooth batter. Stir in the oil, then set aside to rest for 30 minutes.

2 Brush a large crêpe pan with a little oil and put over a medium heat. Pour in a ladleful of batter and fry until set. Flip the crêpe over and quickly fry the other side. Set aside and keep warm. Repeat with the remaining batter.

3 For the filling, preheat the broiler. Put the sliced bananas on to a nonstick baking sheet. Sprinkle with the confectioners' sugar and cook under the broiler for 3–4 minutes until golden. Fill each crêpe with a few banana slices, and top with a spoonful of whipped cream. Fold the crêpes in half or quarters and serve immediately.

Chocolate & Toffee Tart

Serves 6–8

2 cups, plus 2 tablespoons flour, plus
   extra for dusting
Pinch of salt
2 tablespoons confectioners' sugar
1½ sticks (12 tablespoons) unsalted
   butter, diced
2 egg yolks
¼ cup cold water
Cocoa powder, for dusting

For the filling

½ cup water
1¾ cups granulated sugar
½ cup light corn syrup
2 sticks (16 tablespoons) unsalted
   butter
1 cup heavy cream
1 teaspoon pure vanilla extract
4 ounces semisweet chocolate, at least
   50 percent cocoa, grated

1 Sift the flour, salt, and confectioners' sugar into a mixing bowl. Add the butter and rub it in until the mixture resembles bread crumbs. Whisk the egg yolks with the cold water. Make a well in the center of the flour and pour in the egg mixture and mix together to form a dough. Knead briefly. Wrap in plastic wrap and let chill for 20 minutes.

2 Roll out the pastry on a lightly floured surface and use to line a 10-inch loose-bottomed tart pan. Prick the dough all over and chill for 10 minutes.

3 Preheat the oven to 375°F. Line the tart shell with parchment paper and fill with baking beans. Bake for 20 minutes, or until golden and crisp. Remove the paper and beans and let cool.

4 For the filling, put the water in a large saucepan. Add the sugar and corn syrup and cook over a low heat until the sugar has dissolved. Increase the heat and let bubble for about 10 minutes until the sauce is a deep caramel color.

5 Add half of the butter together with the cream and vanilla extract and stand back—it will bubble up. Stir until the mixture is smooth. Pour into the tart shell and chill for 2 hours until set and firm.

6 Melt the chocolate with the remaining butter in a heatproof bowl set over a saucepan of simmering water. Let stand for 15 minutes.

7 Pour the chocolate mixture over the top of the tart, spreading it evenly with a spatula. Chill for at least 1 hour to set, then dust with cocoa powder.

Chocolate Tiramisù

Serves 8–10

8 ounces good-quality white chocolate, broken into pieces
½ cup milk
3 eggs, separated
½ cup granulated sugar
2 pounds mascarpone cheese
½ cup Marsala wine
8 ounces amaretti cookies

For the white chocolate curls
4 ounces good-quality white chocolate

1 Put the chocolate and milk in a heatproof bowl set over a saucepan of simmering water. Heat until the chocolate has melted, then remove from the heat, stir until smooth and let cool.

2 Put the egg yolks and sugar in a bowl and whisk until light and frothy. Beat in the cooled chocolate mixture.

3 Spoon the mascarpone into a large mixing bowl and carefully beat in the chocolate mixture. Don't overwork the mascarpone or it will separate.

4 With clean beaters, beat the egg whites in a clean, grease-free bowl until soft peaks form, then fold into the mascarpone mixture. Spoon half the mixture into a serving dish.

5 Pour the Marsala wine into a shallow bowl and dip both sides of the amaretti cookies in for about 10 seconds, then arrange on top of the mascarpone mixture. Spoon the remaining mascarpone mixture over and let chill for at least 3-4 hours.

6 To make the white chocolate curls, melt the chocolate as in step 1, then spread very thinly over a marble slab or work surface. Let cool until just hard, then draw the blade of a small sharp knife across the surface, keeping it at a slight angle—the chocolate should roll into curls. Put on parchment paper in the refrigerator to set hard, then arrange over the top of the tiramisù.

Cappuccino Truffle Cake

Makes 6–8 slices

1 tablespoon instant coffee powder
⅔ cup boiling water
⅔ cup pitted prunes, chopped
¼ cup Tia Maria or other coffee liqueur
1 stick (8 tablespoons) unsalted butter,
  plus extra for greasing
6 ounces semisweet chocolate, broken
  into squares
5 eggs, separated
½ cup granulated sugar
1 teaspoon pure vanilla extract
1 tablespoon cornstarch
Cocoa powder, for dusting

1 Dissolve the coffee powder in the boiling water in a small cup, then pour over the prunes in a bowl. Stir in the liqueur. Soak overnight.

2 Preheat the oven to 325°F. Grease and line an 8-inch springform cake pan.

3 Melt the butter and chocolate in a heatproof bowl set over a saucepan of hot water. Remove from the heat.

4 Using a hand-held electric mixer, beat the egg yolks and sugar together in a separate heatproof bowl set over a saucepan of simmering water, until the mixture is very thick and creamy. Remove from the heat.

5 Drain any excess liquid from the prunes. Stir the vanilla extract, drained prunes, and melted chocolate into the creamy mixture and set aside.

6 With clean beaters, beak the egg whites in a clean, grease-free bowl until stiff. Beat in the cornstarch, then fold this into the chocolate mixture. Pour the mixture evenly into the prepared pan. Bake in the oven for 50 minutes, or until it is springy to the touch.

7 Remove the cake from the oven and let cool completely in the pan. Turn the cake out on to a serving plate and dust with cocoa powder. Serve in slices.

Chocolate Amaretto

Cheesecake

Makes 10–12 slices

3 tablespoons unsalted butter, melted,
  plus extra for greasing
1½ cups graham cracker crumbs
3–4 amaretti cookies, crumbled
½ teaspoon pure almond extract
½ teaspoon ground cinnamon
White chocolate curls, to decorate

For the filling

12 ounces good-quality white
  chocolate, broken into squares
½ cup whipping cream
Three 8-ounce packages cream cheese
⅓ cup granulated sugar
4 eggs
2 tablespoons Amaretto liqueur or
  ½ teaspoon pure almond extract
½ teaspoon pure vanilla extract

For the topping

1¾ cups sour cream
¼ cup granulated sugar
1 tablespoon Amaretto or
  ½ teaspoon pure almond extract

1 Preheat the oven to 350°F. Grease a 9-inch springform cake pan. Combine the graham cracker and amaretti crumbs in a mixing bowl. Add the butter and flavorings. Press the mixture in the base and on sides of the pan. Bake for 5 minutes, then transfer to a wire rack. Reduce the temperature to 300°F.

2 Melt the chocolate and cream in a saucepan over a low heat until smooth. Beat the cheese in a bowl until smooth. Gradually add the sugar, then beat in each egg. Slowly beat in the chocolate mix, Amaretto, and vanilla. Spoon over the base. Put on a baking sheet and bake for 45–55 minutes until the edge is firm, but the center is slightly soft. Increase the temperature to 400°F.

3 Beat the topping ingredients together. Spread over the cheesecake and bake for 5–7 minutes. Turn off the oven, but leave the cheesecake inside for 1 hour. Transfer to a wire rack. Run a knife around the edge of the cheesecake, but leave in the pan. Chill overnight. Remove the cheesecake from the pan and decorate with chocolate shavings. Serve in slices.

Chocolate Pudding

Serves 4–6

¾ cup, plus 2 tablespoons granulated
sugar

¼ cup cornstarch

¼ teaspoon salt

¼ teaspoon ground cinnamon
(optional)

1⅔ cups milk

½ cup whipping cream

¹⁄₂ stick (4 tablespoons) butter, cut into
pieces

3 ounces semisweet chocolate, chopped

1 egg

1 teaspoon pure vanilla extract

To decorate
Whipped cream
Chocolate shavings

1 Stir together the sugar, cornstarch, salt and
cinnamon, if using, in a large heavy-based
saucepan and gradually whisk in the milk and
cream. Add the butter and chocolate and set over
medium heat. Cook until the chocolate melts and
the mixture thickens, whisking frequently. Bring to
a boil and boil for 1 minute. Remove the pan from
the heat.

2 Beat the egg in a small bowl. Stir in a spoonful
of the hot chocolate mixture, whisking
continuously. Slowly pour the egg into the
chocolate mixture, whisking continuously to
prevent lumps from forming—the mixture will be
very thick. Remove from the heat.

3 Strain the mixture into a large glass measuring
cup, pressing to push the thick mixture
through, and stir in the vanilla extract.

4 Pour or spoon the pudding into dessert
dishes, custard cups or ramekins and cool. Cover
and chill for 2 hours, or overnight. Decorate with
whipped cream and a few chocolate shavings on top.

Peppermint Chocolate
Layer Cake

Makes 10–12 slices

⅔ stick (5 tablespoons) unsalted butter,
  plus extra for greasing
6 ounces semisweet chocolate, broken
  into squares
2½ cups granulated sugar
3 egg yolks
1½ cups milk
2⅓ cups self-rising flour
Pinch of salt
¼ teaspoon baking soda
2 teaspoons pure vanilla extract

For the icing
3 egg whites
2 cups granulated sugar
Pinch of salt
¼ teaspoon cream of tartar
3 tablespoons water
2–3 drops of green food coloring
2–3 drops of peppermint flavoring
⅓ cup crushed peppermints

1 Preheat the oven to 350°F. Grease and line two 8-inch round sandwich cake pans with parchment paper. Melt the chocolate and butter in a heatproof bowl set over a saucepan of simmering water. Let cool to room temperature. Stir in the sugar, then add the egg yolks and half of the milk and mix well.

2 Add the flour, salt, and baking soda and beat for 1 minute using a hand-held electric mixer. Beat in the remaining milk and the vanilla extract. Spoon the mixture into the prepared pans, dividing it evenly, and level the surface. Bake for 25–30 minutes, or until just firm to the touch. Turn out on to a wire rack and let cool.

3 For the icing, mix the egg whites, sugar, salt, cream of tartar, and water in a heatproof bowl set over a saucepan of simmering water. Whisk for 7 minutes, or until firm peaks form. Remove the bowl from the heat and stir in the food coloring and peppermint flavoring. Sandwich the two cakes together with some icing, then spread the remaining icing evenly over the top and sides of the cake. Decorate with the crushed peppermints.

Double Chocolate Chunky

Brownies

Serves 6

1 stick (8 tablespoons) butter, diced,
plus extra for greasing
16 ounces semisweet chocolate
1 teaspoon instant coffee powder
1 tablespoon hot water
3 large eggs
¾ cup, plus 2 tablespoons granulated
sugar
1 teaspoon pure vanilla extract
⅔ cup self-rising flour
1⅓ cups pecans, broken into pieces

Tip
Try not to overcook
the brownies, otherwise
the soft, gooey texture
will be spoiled.

1 Preheat the oven to 375°F. Grease and line an 8 x 12-inch baking pan with parchment paper.

2 Chop 6 ounces of the chocolate into chunks and set aside. Put the rest in a bowl with the butter and melt slowly over a saucepan of simmering water. Stir until smooth, then let cool. Meanwhile, dissolve the coffee in the hot water.

3 Lightly whisk the eggs, coffee, sugar, and vanilla extract together in a bowl. Gradually whisk in the chocolate and butter mixture, then fold in the flour, nuts, and chocolate chunks. Pour into the prepared pan. Bake for 35–40 minutes, or until firm to the touch.

4 Let cool for 5 minutes, then cut into squares. Cool in the pan before removing from the parchment paper. Dust with cocoa powder before serving.

Super-quick Bailey's
Chocolate Mousse

Serves 2

2 ounces semisweet chocolate

4 ounces mascarpone cheese

3 tablespoons Bailey's Irish Cream
   liqueur

Tip

To make a really
indulgent Bailey's sundae, layer
spoonfuls of the set mousse and
scoops of chocolate and vanilla ice
cream in a tall glass, then sprinkle
chopped toasted nuts
over the top and
serve immediately.

1 Break the chocolate into pieces and put in a heatproof bowl set over a saucepan of simmering water. Stir occasionally until the chocolate has melted. Let cool slightly.

2 Meanwhile, put the mascarpone and Bailey's in a bowl and beat together until smooth and creamy. Stir in the cooled melted chocolate and chill for at least 30 minutes before serving.

Chocolate & Brandy

Truffles

Makes 20–30

8 ounces semisweet chocolate
1 tablespoon brandy
1⅓ cups heavy cream
¼ stick (2 tablespoons) unsalted butter,
  cut into cubes
Cocoa powder for dusting

1 Break the chocolate into small pieces and put in a bowl with the brandy.

2 Heat the cream in a saucepan and bring to the boil. Pour over the chocolate, stirring, until the mixture is smooth and glossy. Add the cubes of butter a few at a time, beating until they are incorporated in the mixture. Chill until the mixture is on the point of setting.

3 Beat the mixture with an electric whisk for 3-4 minutes until light and fluffy. Return to the refrigerator to firm up completely.

4 Scoop out teaspoons of the truffle mixture, roll into balls and dust in the cocoa powder.

Chocolate Layer Cake

Makes 10 slices

Butter, for greasing

1¾ cups all-purpose flour, plus extra
   for dusting

1½ teaspoons baking soda

½ teaspoon baking powder

1 teaspoon salt

¾ cup granulated sugar

2 teaspoons pure vanilla extract

1⅓ cups buttermilk

½ cup, plus 1 tablespoon shortening

3 eggs

2½ ounces plain chocolate, melted and
   cooled

Chocolate leaves or curls, to decorate
   (optional)

For the fudgy icing

1 cup heavy cream

15 ounces good-quality semisweet
   chocolate, chopped

⅔ stick (5 tablespoons) unsalted butter,
   at room temperature

1 tablespoon pure vanilla extract

1 Preheat the oven to 350°F. Grease and flour two 9-inch round cake pans.

2 Sift the flour, baking soda, baking powder, and salt into a mixing bowl. Add the sugar, vanilla extract, buttermilk, shortening, eggs, and cooled melted chocolate. Using a hand-held electric mixer on low speed, begin to beat the mixture slowly until the ingredients are blended, then increase the mixer speed to high and beat for 5 minutes, scraping down the sides of the bowl.

3 Spoon the mixture into the pans, dividing it evenly, then level the surface. Bake for 25 minutes, or until the tops are set. Cool in the pans for 10 minutes, then turn out on to a wire rack and let cool completely.

4 For the icing, pour the cream into a saucepan and bring to a boil over a medium-high heat. Remove from the heat and add the chocolate, stirring, until melted and smooth. Beat in the butter and vanilla until well combined. Chill, stirring every 10–15 minutes, until the icing becomes quite thick and spreadable. Remove from the refrigerator and continue to stir occasionally until the icing is thick.

5 Put one cake, top-side up, on a plate and spread with about a quarter of the icing. Put the second cake on top, flat-side up, then spread the top and sides of the cake with the remaining icing. Decorate with chocolate leaves or curls, if liked.

COOL & CREAMY

- Lychee Sorbet
- Blue Lagoon Ice Cream
- Apricot Bavarois
- Raspberry Swirl Shortbread Sandwiches
- Vanilla Ice Cream & Hot Chocolate Sauce
- Deluxe Banana Split
- Mandarin Paradise Parfait
- Creamy Zabaglione
- Lemon Surprise Pudding
- Rose-scented Panacotta
- Cheesecake Deluxe
- Vanilla Cream Napoleon
- Grasshopper Soufflés
- Raspberry Mousse
- Sweethearts
- Caribbean Coconut Trifle
- Fig & Armagnac Ice Cream
- Fresh Orange Ice Cream Cake
- Gluten-free Fruit Roll
- Coffee Cheesecake with Pecan Sauce
- Strawberry Ice Cream Angelfood Cake
- Berries Jubilee Sundae
- Ice Cream Pie
- Exotic Iced Delight
- Ice Cream Cake
- Red Currant Swirl
- Black Currant & White Rum Fool

CHAPTER THREE

COOL &
CREAMY

Lychee Sorbet

Serves 2

6 tablespoons granulated sugar
1 cup water
14-ounce can lychees in syrup
1 tablespoon lemon juice
1 egg white

Tip

Elderflower cordial adds a wonderful, scented flavor to this refreshing sorbet, but if it's hard to find, lemonade will have a similar effect. Whisked egg whites are added to lighten the texture.

1 Heat the sugar and water together in a saucepan until the sugar has dissolved. Bring to a boil and simmer for 1 minute. Remove from the heat and let cool.

2 Purée the lychees and syrup in a food processor or blender, then pass through a strainer, pressing down well to extract all the juice. Add the lemon juice.

3 Pour the mixture into a shallow freezerproof container and freeze for about 2–3 hours until just beginning to hold its shape.

4 Whisk the egg white in a clean, grease-free bowl until soft peaks form, then add to the sorbet. Continue freezing and whisking by hand until it becomes thick and creamy, then freeze until required.

5 Remove from the freezer and put in the refrigerator for 5–10 minutes before serving.

Blue Lagoon Ice Cream

Serves 6

⅔ cup milk
½ vanilla bean
2 egg yolks
5 tablespoons granulated sugar
2 cups blueberries
1 tablespoon water
1 tablespoon white rum
1 cup heavy cream
2 small store-bought meringues

1 Put the milk and vanilla bean in a saucepan and bring to almost boiling point over a low heat. Remove from the heat and take out the vanilla bean. Using a hand-held electric mixer, whisk the egg yolks and 4 tablespoons of the sugar until pale and slightly thickened, then lightly whisk in the milk.

2 Return to a clean heavy-based, nonstick saucepan. Cook over a low heat, stirring continuously, until the mixture thickens to the consistency of heavy cream and coats the back of a spoon. Cover with plastic wrap and let cool. Meanwhile, cook the blueberries with the rest of the sugar and the water for 2 minutes until softened. Let cool, then stir in the rum.

3 Whip the cream in a bowl until stiff peaks form and fold into the cold custard. Pour into a shallow freezerproof container and freeze for about 2–3 hours, or until half-frozen. Using a hand-held electric mixer, beat the mixture to break down any ice crystals. Repeat this process at least twice until the ice cream holds its shape. Alternatively, churn in an ice cream maker.

4 Swirl the meringues through the ice cream, followed quickly by the blueberry sauce, to make a marbled pattern. Spoon into a clean freezerproof container and freeze until firm. Remove from the freezer 20–30 minutes before serving.

Tip
If you want to make plain vanilla ice cream, omit the blueberry sauce and meringues, and freeze. Or, if you want to use any other fruit or chocolate sauce, swirl them in, as for the blueberries, at the end.

Apricot Bavarois

Serves 6

3 cups apricots, halved
2 tablespoons water
1 tablespoon lemon juice
1 cup granulated sugar
½ cup milk
2 tablespoons water
1 tablespoon powdered gelatin
3 eggs, separated
¾ cup heavy cream
Whipped cream and chocolate curls, to
   decorate

1 Put the apricots in a pan and add the water. Cover and cook gently for 15–20 minutes, until the fruit is soft and pulpy. Remove from the heat and scoop out the pits. Process the fruit with the lemon juice in a food processor, press through a strainer into a bowl, then measure it. There should be 1 cup. If not, add a little fresh orange juice to top up. Stir in 2 tablespoons of the sugar.

2 Put the rest of the sugar in a heatproof bowl and stir in the milk, with the sweetened apricot purée. Put the water in a cup and sprinkle the gelatin on top. Leave until spongy. Place the heatproof bowl over a pan of simmering water and stir until the sugar has dissolved, then add the gelatin and continue stirring until that has dissolved, too.

3 In a small bowl, beat the egg yolks with a little of the apricot mixture, then add the mixture to the heatproof bowl. Continue to stir over the heat for about 5 minutes, until the mixture thickens slightly. Let cool, so that it starts to thicken.

4 Whisk the egg whites until soft peaks form. Whip the cream lightly. Fold first the cream and then the egg whites into the apricot mixture, and spoon into a 6-cup dessert bowl. Chill for 3–4 hours, until set. Decorate with whipped cream and chocolate curls.

Raspberry Swirl
Shortbread Sandwiches

Serves 2

4 round shortbread cookies
2 scoops raspberry swirl ice cream

To decorate (optional)
Fresh berries
Confectioners' sugar

1 Put 2 of the shortbread cookies on a serving plate and place a scoop of raspberry swirl ice cream on top. Carefully balance the other shortbread cookies on top of the ice cream.

2 Pile fresh summer berries on top of the sandwiches and dust with confectioners' sugar, if liked. Serve at once and eat before the ice cream melts!

Tip
If you fancy something less fruity, why not try plain vanilla ice cream or for something a little sweeter replace the raspberry ripple ice cream with chocolate.

Vanilla Ice Cream

& Hot Chocolate Sauce

Serves 2

1⅓ cups milk
1 vanilla bean, split lengthwise
    or 1 teaspoon pure vanilla extract
5 egg yolks
½ cup granulated sugar
1⅓ cups heavy cream

For the hot chocolate sauce
4 ounces bittersweet chocolate,
    chopped
1⅓ cups heavy cream

1 For the ice cream, put the milk and vanilla bean into a saucepan and bring slowly to boiling point, stirring frequently. Remove from the heat and let infuse for 15 minutes. Meanwhile, whisk the egg yolks and sugar until thick and pale. Remove the vanilla bean, if using, and pour the milk mixture onto the eggs and sugar, whisking all the time.

2 Return this mixture to a clean saucepan and put over a low heat. Stir continuously with a wooden spoon, until the mixture thickens. Do not allow to boil or the egg will scramble. The custard is ready when the mixture coats the back of a wooden spoon without running off freely. Once the custard has cooled, chill until cold.

3 Whip the cream in a bowl until soft peaks form, then fold into the chilled custard. Pour this mixture into a freezerproof container. Cover and freeze for 2 hours. Remove from the freezer and beat the mixture using an electric mixer or wire whisk until smooth. Repeat freezing and whisking twice, then freeze until firm. The whisking during freezing prevents large ice crystals forming and ensures that the ice cream is smooth.

4 Put the chocolate into a heatproof bowl. Bring the cream to boiling point in a saucepan, then remove from the heat and leave for a minute to allow it to come off the boil. Pour the cream over the chocolate. Let stand for about 1 minute, then stir until smooth. Use immediately as needed.

Deluxe Banana Split

Serves 2

2 scoops each vanilla, chocolate, and strawberry ice cream

2 ripe bananas

½ cup whipping cream, whipped and chilled

⅓ cup chopped pecans

2 maraschino cherries, drained

For the fudge sauce

1 cup, plus 2 tablespoons caster sugar

1 cup whipping cream

1 tablespoon light corn syrup

4 ounces semisweet chocolate, chopped

2 tablespoons butter, diced

1 teaspoon pure vanilla extract

For the hot butterscotch sauce

1 cup light brown sugar

1 cup whipping cream

2 tablespoons light corn syrup

2 tablespoons butter, diced

1 teaspoon rum extract

1 For the fudge sauce, heat the sugar, cream, corn syrup, and semisweet chocolate in a medium, heavy-based saucepan over a medium-high heat, stirring frequently, until the chocolate is melted and the sauce boils. Reduce the heat and stir in the butter and vanilla extract until smooth. Keep warm or let cool to room temperature.

2 For the hot butterscotch sauce, put the brown sugar, cream and corn syrup in another saucepan and bring to a boil over a medium-high heat. Boil for 2 minutes, then reduce the heat. Beat in the butter and simmer for a further 2 minutes, or until thickened. Stir in the rum extract and remove from the heat; cover and keep warm.

3 Soften the 3 ice creams to room temperature if necessary, for about 5 minutes. Split each banana in half along its length. Lay two halves in each dish, forming a V-shape. Arrange a scoop of each ice cream along each split banana. Spoon a little of the fudge sauce over the chocolate and strawberry ice creams, and spoon the butterscotch sauce over the vanilla.

4 Pipe or spoon whipped cream over the ice cream, sprinkle with chopped pecans and top with a cherry. Serve the extra sauces separately.

Mandarin Paradise Parfait

Serves 4

10-ounce can mandarin oranges
2½-ounce packet orange-flavored jello
6 ounces cream cheese, softened

To decorate
Whipped cream
Fresh citrus and ripe passion fruits

1 Drain the mandarins and reserve the juice. Add boiling water to the juice to make 1½ cups of liquid and dissolve the jello in it. Hand-beat the cream cheese until smooth and creamy. Slowly add ½ cup of the jello, beating thoroughly to avoid lumps.

2 Cut the mandarins up roughly and add to the cream cheese mixture. Pour half of the remaining jello mixture into 4 tall glasses and put in the coldest part of the refrigerator to set for 3–4 hours. When ready, pour the soft cheese mixture into the parfait glasses on top of the set jello and set, as above. Using the leftover jello mixture, add the final layer.

3 Chop a selection of citrus fruits, such as oranges, grapefruit and clementines, squeezing over them the juice and seeds of 1 or 2 passion fruits. Use to decorate the parfaits or serve in a separate bowl for a refreshing and colorful fruit salad accompaniment.

Creamy Zabaglione

Serves 4

4 egg yolks
¼ cup granulated sugar
6 tablespoons Marsala wine
Grated zest of ½ lemon
⅔ cup heavy cream, whipped
½ teaspoon pure vanilla extract
Ladyfingers or biscotti to serve

Tip

Beating over hot water heats up the mixture and lets the egg yolks cook and thicken the mixture. Take care though—if it overheats, it will separate.

1 Put the egg yolks and sugar into a bowl and whisk over simmering water with an electric hand-held mixer until the mixture is pale yellow, creamy and smooth.

2 Add the Marsala a little at a time, whisking continuously until the mixture is very light and almost thick enough to leave a trail when the beaters are lifted.

3 Remove the bowl from the heat and beat for a further 5 minutes. Fold in the lemon zest, whipped cream, and vanilla extract and serve in glasses with ladyfingers or biscotti to dip in.

Lemon Surprise Pudding

Serves 4

3 tablespoons butter, softened,
   plus extra for greasing
½ cup, plus 2 tablespoons sugar
Finely grated zest and juice of 2 large
   lemons
2 eggs, separated
6 tablespoons self-rising flour
¾ cup milk
Light cream, to serve

1 Preheat the oven to 350°F. Grease a 1-quart pudding basin or baking dish and set aside.

2 Beat the butter, sugar, and lemon zest together until well mixed. Next beat in the egg yolks, a little at a time. Fold in the flour, alternating with the milk and lemon juice. Finally, beat the egg whites in a clean, grease-free bowl and fold them into the mixture. At this stage, the mixture will look curdled, but this is to be expected.

3 Pour the mixture into the prepared pudding basin or baking dish and bake in the center of the oven for 40–45 minutes until golden brown and risen. Serve hot with fresh cream.

Rose-scented Panacotta

Serves 2

2 leaves gelatin
3 tablespoons milk
2 cups whipping cream
2 tablespoons granulated sugar
1 tablespoon rosewater
Fresh rose petals, to decorate

1 Soak the gelatin in the milk until soft. Put the cream, sugar, and rosewater in a small saucepan and heat gently until almost boiling. Remove from the heat and let cool. Add the milk from the gelatin and, once cooled, add the gelatin itself. Stir until completely dissolved.

2 Pour the mixture into two ¾ cup dariole molds or pudding basins. Cover and refrigerate overnight. Unmold, decorate with rose petals, and serve.

Tip
If the panacotta is proving difficult to remove from the molds, briefly dip the base of the molds in boiling water.

Cheesecake Deluxe

Serves 4

For the crust
1¾ cups graham cracker crumbs
3 tablespoons granulated sugar
1 teaspoon ground cinnamon
½ teaspoon freshly grated nutmeg
⅔ stick (5½ tablespoons) butter

For the filling
⅓ stick (3 tablespoons) butter
½ cup granulated sugar
⅛ teaspoon salt
1 tablespoon grated lemon zest
3 large eggs, separated
Juice of 1 lemon
½ teaspoon pure vanilla extract
Two 8-ounce tubs cream cheese
1 cup sour cream

1 Preheat the oven to 300°F. To make the crust, combine the cracker crumbs with the sugar, cinnamon, and nutmeg. Melt the butter, blend it into the crumb mixture, and pack firmly against the base and sides of a 9-inch springform cake pan or ovenproof glass dish. Let chill until required.

2 For the filling, cream the butter, sugar, salt, and lemon zest together in a bowl. Slowly beat the egg yolks into the creamed mixture. Add the lemon juice, vanilla extract, cream cheese, and sour cream. Whisk the egg whites in a clean, grease-free bowl until soft peaks form. Fold into the other ingredients and ladle onto the base.

3 Bake the cheesecake for 1–1¼ hours until firm. Let cool in the pan, then remove from the pan and onto a serving plate. Chill for several hours in the refrigerator before serving.

Vanilla Cream Napoleon

Serves 8

12 ounces puff pastry, thawed if frozen
3 tablespoons confectioners' sugar

For the filling
2 cups milk
1 vanilla bean
1 teaspoon pure vanilla extract
5 egg yolks
½ cup, plus 2 tablespoons granulated
  sugar
1 tablespoon all-purpose flour
1 tablespoon cornstarch
1 cup heavy cream
2¾ cups strawberries, thinly sliced

1 Roll out the puff pastry dough to a rectangle 12 x 8½ inches. Halve lengthwise and put on a nonstick baking sheet. Sift the confectioners' sugar over one half of the dough and score into diamond shapes using the tip of a sharp knife. Chill for 30 minutes.

2 Preheat the oven to 400°F. Bake the pastry halves for 15–20 minutes until puffed and golden. Cool, then split the unsugared pastry horizontally, discarding the top. Split the sugared half horizontally, reserving both pieces.

3 Put the milk, vanilla bean, and vanilla extract into a large saucepan and slowly bring to a boil. Whisk the egg yolks with the sugar, flour, and cornstarch. Add the hot milk and mix well. Remove the vanilla bean and scrape out the seeds, stirring them into the custard. Cook, stirring, for 4–5 minutes until the custard has thickened. Cover with plastic wrap and let cool completely.

4 Whip the cream until soft peaks form and fold into the cooled custard. Spread half of the custard over the unsugared piece of pastry and cover with half the strawberries.

5 Put the base of the split sugared piece over the fruit and press down. Spread the remaining custard over and top with the rest of the strawberries. Put the sugared pastry on top.

Grasshopper Soufflés

Serves 2

2 envelopes unflavored gelatin
2 cups water
1 cup granulated sugar
4 medium eggs, separated
8-ounce tub cream cheese, softened
¼ cup crème de menthe
1 cup heavy cream, whipped

To decorate
Candied flowers
Fresh mint leaves

1 Put the gelatin with ½ cup of water in a saucepan. Add the remaining 1½ cups of water when it is softened. Stir over a low heat until dissolved. Remove from the heat and blend in ¾ cup of the sugar and lightly beaten egg yolks. Return to the heat and simmer for 2–3 minutes. Remove from the heat and set to one side.

2 Put the softened cream cheese in a large mixing bowl. Beat with an electric mixer. Gradually add the cooked mixture to the cream cheese, mixing until well blended. Stir in the crème de menthe. Chill for 15 minutes until slightly thickened.

3 Whisk the egg whites in a clean bowl until soft peaks form. Gradually add the remaining ½ cup of sugar, beating until stiff peaks form. Fold into the chilled cream cheese mixture. Fold in the whipped cream (reserve a small amount for decoration, if desired).

4 Wrap 3-inch collars of aluminum foil around the rims of the four soufflé dishes, so that the foil extends beyond the rims of the dishes, and secure with tape. Pour the mixture into the dishes and chill for 1 hour until firm. Remove the foil collars before serving. Decorate with candied flowers and mint leaves.

Raspberry Mousse

Serves 6

5 cups fresh raspberries
2 tablespoons confectioners' sugar
2 tablespoons lemon juice
¼ cup water
1 tablespoon powdered gelatin
2 eggs, plus 1 egg yolk
6 tablespoons sugar
1 cup heavy cream
Whipped cream, to decorate

1 Set aside a few raspberries for decoration. Put the rest in a food processor or blender and add the confectioners' sugar and lemon juice. Process to a purée, then remove the seeds by pressing the purée through a strainer placed over a bowl.

2 Pour the water into a metal measuring cup and sprinkle with the gelatin on top. When it is spongy, set the cup over simmering water until the gelatin melts.

3 Meanwhile, place the eggs, egg yolk, and sugar in the top of a double boiler. Whisk over simmering water until the mixture is very thick, then remove from the heat and gently fold in the gelatin mixture, with 1 cup of the raspberry purée. Save the remaining purée for a sauce.

4 Whip the heavy cream to soft peaks and fold it into the mixture. Spoon into a glass bowl and chill for 3–4 hours, until set.

5 Decorate with whipped cream and the reserved raspberries. Taste the raspberry sauce and add a little extra sugar if you like. Serve with the mousse.

Sweethearts

Serves 2

4 ounces good-quality white chocolate,
  broken into pieces
1 tablespoon light corn syrup
1 tablespoon brandy
⅔ cup heavy cream
2 fresh strawberries, to serve

For the strawberry sauce
1 cup strawberries, hulled
1 tablespoon confectioners' sugar, plus
  extra for dusting

1 Put the chocolate in a heatproof bowl. Add the corn syrup and brandy. Put the bowl over a saucepan of gently simmering water and melt the chocolate, stirring the mixture occasionally.

2 Remove from the heat and let cool slightly. Whip the cream in a bowl until soft peaks form and carefully fold it into the chocolate mixture. Spoon into two ½-cup heart-shaped molds and let set in the refrigerator for at least 2 hours.

3 For the sauce, put the strawberries and confectioners' sugar in a food processor or blender and process until puréed. Press through a strainer to remove the seeds.

4 Run a knife gently around the edge of each chocolate heart, then carefully invert the molds and transfer onto 2 dessert plates. Drizzle the sauce around the hearts and decorate with the fresh strawberries. Dust with extra confectioners' sugar.

Caribbean Coconut Trifle

Serves 2

12 ounces fresh pineapple chunks
1⅓ cups heavy cream
¼ cup coconut milk
¾ cup crème fraîche
¼ cup confectioners' sugar
2 papaya, peeled, seeded, and chopped
2 mangoes, peeled, pitted, and
   chopped
Juice of 1 lime
Toasted flaked coconut, to decorate

Tip
As an extra treat, add a splash of rum to the mix to give it that extra kick.

1 Put the pineapple chunks in a food processor or blender and process briefly until chopped. Transfer to a strainer set over a bowl to drain. Reserve the juice if you wish.

2 Whip the cream in a large bowl until soft peaks form, then lightly fold in the coconut milk, crème fraîche, and confectioners' sugar.

3 Fold the drained pineapple into the cream mixture. Put the papaya and mango in a large serving bowl and pour over the lime juice and ¼ cup of the drained pineapple juice.

4 Spoon the pineapple cream on top of the fruit and scatter over the toasted coconut flakes.

Fig & Armagnac Ice Cream

Serves 4–6

1 pound ripe fresh figs, cut into
    quarters
3 tablespoons Armagnac or brandy
1⅓ cups milk
4 egg yolks
1 cup granulated sugar
1⅓ cups heavy cream
1 teaspoon pure vanilla extract
Fresh figs, cut into slices, to serve

1 Put the figs in a food processor or blender with the Armagnac or brandy and process to a purée. Meanwhile, heat the milk in a saucepan over a low heat until almost boiling.

2 Whisk the egg yolks with ⅔ cup of the sugar with a hand-held electric mixer until pale and slightly thickened, then lightly whisk in the hot milk.

3 Return to a clean, nonstick saucepan. Cook over a low heat, stirring continuously, until the mixture thickens to the consistency of heavy cream and coats the back of a spoon. Cover with plastic wrap and let cool.

4 Lightly whip the cream in a bowl until soft peaks form, then fold it into the cold custard with the puréed figs and vanilla extract. Taste the mixture and add the remaining sugar, if needed.

5 Pour into a shallow freezerproof container and freeze until half-frozen, about 2–3 hours, then beat with a hand-held electric mixer to break down any ice crystals. Repeat this process at least twice more until the ice cream holds its shape. Alternatively, churn in an ice cream maker.

6 Remove from the freezer 20–30 minutes before serving. Serve in scoops with slices of fresh figs.

Tip
The more ripe and flavorful the figs that you use, the better this sophisticated ice cream will taste.

Fresh Orange
Ice Cream Cake

Serves 8

4 oranges
5 eggs, separated
2⅓ cups granulated sugar
2 cups heavy cream
4 ounces ladyfingers
⅓ cup Grand Marnier

1 Line a 9-inch springform pan with plastic wrap.

2 Carefully cut the peel off one orange, removing as much of the white pith as possible. Cut between the separating membranes and lift out the segments. Arrange around the base of the springform pan.

3 Grate the zest of the remaining 3 oranges and set aside. Squeeze the juice from the 3 oranges into a saucepan. Bring to a boil and cook until reduced by half.

4 Put the egg yolks in a large bowl with 1⅓ cups of the sugar and beat with a hand-held electric mixer until thick and frothy. Whisk in the reduced orange juice and grated zest and let cool. Lightly whip the cream in another bowl, then fold into the orange custard.

5 Beat the egg whites in a clean, grease-free bowl until stiff peaks form and beat in the remaining 1 cup of sugar, a tablespoon at a time. Next, fold the mixture into the orange cream.

6 Pour half the mixture over the orange segments in the springform pan. Dip the ladyfingers into the Grand Marnier and arrange in a layer across the orange cream. Spoon the remaining mixture over, cover, and freeze for 7–8 hours.

7 Invert the frozen orange cake on to a serving plate and put in the refrigerator for 30 minutes before serving.

Gluten-free Fruit Roll

Makes 8–10 slices

Butter, for greasing
4 eggs, separated
¾ cup confectioners' sugar, plus extra
   for dusting
1 tablespoon orange flower water
⅓ cup rice flour
⅓ cup potato flour
1 teaspoon gluten-free baking powder

For the filling
1⅓ cups plain yogurt
½ large mango, peeled, pitted, and
   chopped
¼ small papaya, peeled, seeded, and
   chopped
1 ripe passion fruit

To decorate
Fresh mango slices
1 ripe passion fruit, cut in half

1 Preheat the oven to 375°F. Grease and line a 13 x 9-inch baking sheet with sides with parchment paper, then grease the paper as well. For the cake, put the egg whites in a clean bowl and whisk until soft peaks form. Sift half of the confectioners' sugar over the top and whisk in. Whisk the egg yolks with the remaining confectioners' sugar in another bowl until the mixture is pale and very thick. Stir in the orange flower water. Sift the flours and baking powder over the top and fold in. Using a metal spoon, fold in the whisked egg whites mixture, one-third at a time.

2 Spoon the mixture onto the baking sheet, spreading it evenly. Bake in the oven for about 12–15 minutes, or until springy to the touch. Sprinkle a little extra sifted confectioners' sugar over a large sheet of parchment paper and turn out the sponge cake onto the paper. Remove the parchment paper, trim off any firm edges, then loosely roll up the cake with the paper inside and let cool on a wire rack. For the filling, carefully unroll the cake and spread the yogurt evenly over the cake. Scatter over the chopped mango and papaya. Halve the passion fruit and spoon the juice and seeds over the fruit.

3 Carefully roll up the cake, put it on a serving plate, and dust with extra sifted confectioners' sugar. Decorate with slices of mango and the juice and seeds of the passion fruit. Serve in slices.

Coffee Cheesecake
with Pecan Sauce

Serves 6

1½ cup graham cracker crumbs
½ sticks (4 tablespoons) unsalted
   butter, melted
1¼ pounds cream cheese
1 cup packed soft brown sugar
1 teaspoon pure vanilla extract
3 eggs
2 tablespoons very strong
   brewed coffee

For the sauce
4 tablespoons unsalted butter
6 tablespoons brown sugar
1 cup heavy cream
1 teaspoon pure vanilla extract
⅔ cup pecans, toasted and
   finely chopped

1 Combine the cracker crumbs and melted butter. Press into the base of an 8-inch springform pan and chill for 20 minutes.

2 Preheat the oven to 350°F. Beat the cream cheese with the sugar and vanilla extract. Add the eggs and beat until smooth. Stir in the coffee, then spoon into the springform pan.

3 Set the pan in a roasting pan half-full of boiling water and cook in the oven for 55 minutes. Turn off the heat and let the cheesecake cool in the oven for 1 hour, then transfer to the refrigerator before serving.

4 For the sauce, melt the butter in a small saucepan and add the sugar, cream, and vanilla extract. Simmer for 10 minutes, then stir in the pecans. Serve warm with the cheesecake.

Tip
Avoid overbeating the mixture. Overbeating incorporates additional air and tends to cause cracking on the surface of the cheesecake.

Strawberry Ice Cream
Angelfood Cake

Serves 6–8

⅓ cup all-purpose flour
2 tablespoons cornstarch
1 cup granulated sugar
7 large egg whites
¾ teaspoon cream of tartar
Pinch of salt
1½ teaspoons pure vanilla extract
Fresh strawberries, to serve

For the filling
¼ cup strawberry jam
2 cups strawberry ice cream

1 Preheat the oven to 350°F. Sift the flour and cornstarch together. Add ⅓ cup sugar and sift together twice.

2 Whisk the egg whites in a clean, grease-free bowl until foamy. Add the cream of tartar and salt and continue whisking until they are stiff.

3 Whisk the remaining sugar into the egg whites a spoonful at a time until stiff peaks form and are glossy. Whisk in the vanilla extract.

4 Fold in the flour in 3 batches, then spoon into a 9-inch springform tube pan. The mixture should come up to the top of the pan. Level the top and bake for 45–50 minutes, or until lightly golden on top and spongy to the touch. Remove from the oven and invert onto a wire rack. Leave in the pan until cool.

5 Remove the cake from the pan and cool. Wash and dry the pan and line with nonstick baking paper. Cut the cake horizontally and return the base to the pan. Spread the jam over the base and top with ice cream, spreading over evenly. Top with the other half and press down lightly. Freeze until firm. Serve topped with fresh strawberries.

Berries Jubilee Sundae

Serves 2

2 teaspoons unflavored gelatin
¼ cup cold water
¾ cup milk
1 vanilla bean
¾ cup granulated sugar
Pinch of salt
3 cups heavy cream, whipped
Nuts, fudge pieces, maraschino
    cherries, and chocolate novelties to
    decorate

For the berry cream

3½ cups hulled strawberries,
    raspberries or blueberrries
1 cup granulated sugar
2 tablespoons unflavored gelatin
2 tablespoons cold water
3 tablespoons boiling water
1 tablespoon lemon juice
2 cups heavy cream, whipped

For the jubilee sauce

10 ounces fresh or frozen pitted sweet
    cherries, at room temperature
¼ cup brandy, slightly warmed
2 tablespoons kirsch

1 For the ice cream, soak the gelatin in ¼ cup cold water for 10 minutes. Boil milk with the vanilla bean in a heavy-based saucepan and leave for 20 minutes. Stir in the sugar and salt, then add the gelatin. Pour into a container and cool, then freeze for 1–2 hours, or until ice crystals start to form and it is firm all the way through. Whisk the mixture until thickened but not stiff, then fold in the cream. Freeze overnight.

2 For the berry cream, put the berries and sugar in a bowl and crush. Let stand for 1 hour. Dissolve the gelatin in the 2 tablespoons of cold water, then add the 3 tablespoons of boiling water. Stir in the crushed berries and the lemon juice. When cool, fold in the whipped cream. Pour into a wet mold and chill overnight.

3 For the jubilee sauce, heat the cherries in a saucepan. Add the brandy and set on fire. When the flames have died down, add the kirsch. Layer the sauce, berry cream, and ice cream into sundae glasses and decorate with nuts, fudge, cherries, and chocolate novelties.

Ice Cream Pie

Serves 6–8

6 ounces chocolate chip cookies, crushed

¾ stick (6 tablespoons) unsalted butter, melted

For the filling
3 cups vanilla ice cream, slightly softened

3 cups chocolate ice cream, slightly softened

For the sauce
5 ounces milk chocolate, broken into pieces

¼ stick (2 tablespoons) unsalted butter

2 tablespoons light corn syrup

3 tablespoons water

2 tablespoons finely chopped hazelnuts

1 Mix the crushed cookies with the melted butter and press the mixture into the base and halfway up the sides of an 8-inch springform pan. Chill for 20 minutes, or until firm.

2 Pile alternate scoops of vanilla and chocolate ice cream over the cookie base, leaving the top quite rough. Freeze for at least 1 hour, or until the ice cream is firm.

3 Meanwhile, make the sauce. Put the chocolate, butter, and corn syrup in a heatproof bowl with the water and melt over a saucepan of gently simmering water. Stir until smooth, then remove from the heat and let cool.

4 Preheat the broiler. Toast the finely chopped hazelnuts under the broiler for 2–3 minutes, or until dark golden.

5 Remove the pie from the pan. Pour the sauce over the ice cream and scatter with the toasted hazelnuts. Freeze until ready to serve, or serve immediately.

Exotic Iced Delight

Serves 2-4

1 large mango, peeled and pitted
1⅓ cups custard sauce (see tip)
1⅓ cups heavy cream

To decorate
Chopped toasted pecans
Maple syrup

1 Put the mango flesh in a food processor and process to a purée. Pour the custard into a bowl and stir in the mango purée. Whip the cream until soft peaks form and fold into the custard mixture.

2 Pour the mixture into a shallow freezerproof container and cover with an airtight lid. Freeze for 1 hour, then beat with a fork to break up any large ice crystals.

3 Return the ice cream to the freezer for 2 hours, then beat again. Finally, return to the freezer for 4 hours, or until frozen. Scoop the ice cream into glasses, sprinkle with toasted pecans and drizzle with maple syrup before serving.

Tip

To make the custard sauce:

Mix 2 teaspoons cornstarch with 2 tablespoons light cream in a cup. Beat 2 egg yolks in a bowl until pale, then stir in the cornstarch mix. Heat 1 cup light cream with 4 tablespoons sugar in a saucepan. When hot, pour half the hot cream on to the egg mixture, stirring, then add the mixture to the remaining hot cream in the pan. Cook for 5 minutes until thick, then stir in ½ teaspoon vanilla extract. Cover and cool.

Ice Cream Cake

Serves 10–12

1½ cups granulated sugar
1 cup cake flour
8 medium egg whites, at room
    temperature
1¼ teaspoons cream of tartar
Pinch of salt
1 teaspoon pure almond extract
½ teaspoon pure vanilla extract
6–8 maraschino cherries (optional)
Confectioners' sugar, for dusting

For the filling
Scoops of ice cream, preferably
    vanilla, enough to fill center core
15-ounce can yellow peaches, drained
Fresh strawberries and raspberries

For the Melba sauce
¾ cup granulated sugar
½ cup water
3½ cups fresh strawberries or
    raspberries, puréed and chilled

1 Preheat the oven to 350°F. Sift the sugar twice. Sift the flour 4 times in a separate bowl. Set both aside. Beat the egg whites in a clean, grease-free bowl until frothy. Add the cream of tartar and salt and continue to whisk until soft peaks forms. Sprinkle 2 tablespoons sugar over the egg white peaks and beat until blended. Repeat the process until the sugar is used up. Beat in the almond and vanilla extracts. With a rubber spatula, fold in the flour, ¼ cup at a time. If using, cut the cherries into quarters and fold into the mixture.

2 Spoon the mixture into an ungreased 12-inch fluted ring mold. Cut through it with a knife to get rid of any air bubbles and level off. Bake in the center of the oven for 40–60 minutes until the top turns light brown.

3 Put all the ingredients for the Melba sauce in a saucepan and bring to a boil, stirring occasionally until the sugar dissolves. Let cool.

4 Remove the cake from the oven, invert on to a wire rack and let cool in the mold for 1 hour. Run a sharp knife around the edges of the mold to loosen the cake before inverting on to a serving plate. Fill the center with ice cream and fruit. Drizzle over the Melba sauce and dust with confectioners' sugar.

Red Currant Swirl

Serves 4–6

1 cup, plus 2 tablespoons granulated
  sugar

2½ cups water

⅔ cup rosé or red wine

4 cups red currants or gooseberries,
  stripped from their stalks

3 tablespoons arrowroot mixed to a
  paste with 3 tablespoons water

4–6 tablespoons sour cream

Tip
Arrowroot is preferable to cornstarch for thickening this particular sauce as it gives a clear, rather than a cloudy, result.

1 Put the sugar and water in a saucepan. Heat, stirring, until the sugar dissolves, then bring to a boil and cook, without stirring for 2–3 minutes. Stir in the wine.

2 Add the red currants or gooseberries to the wine syrup, reduce the heat, and poach them for about 10 minutes until just tender.

3 Stir in the arrowroot paste. Bring to a boil, stirring continuously until the mixture thickens. Let cool, then chill for several hours. Serve in individual glass dishes, swirling 1 tablespoon of sour cream on the surface of each portion.

Black Currant
& White Rum Fool

Serves 4

15 ounces fresh or frozen black
  currants
¹/₄ cup granulated sugar
2 tablespoons fresh orange juice
2 tablespoons white rum
1¹/₃ cups heavy cream, lightly whipped

For the custard
²/₃ cup whole milk
½ vanilla bean
2 egg yolks
¼ cup granulated sugar

1 Make a purée by cooking the fruit, sugar, and orange juice in a covered saucepan until very soft for 5 minutes. Let cool, then purée in a food processor or blender. Push the juice and pulp through a strainer. Stir in the white rum and set aside.

2 For the custard, heat the milk and vanilla bean together over a low heat until the milk almost boils. Remove from the heat and remove the vanilla bean. Whisk the egg yolks and sugar together until pale and slightly thickened, then whisk in the milk.

3 Return the mixture to a heavy-based nonstick saucepan. Cook over a low heat, stirring continuously, until the mixture thickens to the consistency of heavy cream. Cover the surface with plastic wrap and let cool.

4 Stir the fruit purée into the custard and then gently fold in the whipped cream. Stir gently until it thickens slightly, then spoon into glasses and chill before serving.

PIES & TARTS

- Raisin Cheese Pie
- Chess Pie
- Coffee & Walnut Pie
- Georgia Pecan Pie
- Freeform Strawberry & Rhubarb Pie
- Strawberry & Custard Tartlets
- Peanut Butter Pie
- Banana Tarte Tatin
- Bourbon Pie
- Fig & Ricotta Tart
- Tarte Fine aux Pommes
- Honey & Mixed Nut Tart
- Orange Chiffon Pie
- Banana Cream Pie

- Marlborough Pie
- Freeform Spiced Plum Pie
- Caramel Cream Pie
- Blacksmith Pie
- Pear Tart with Walnut & Star Anise
- Chocolate Chip & Peanut Butter Pie
- Frangipani Cream Pie
- Figgy Meringue Tarts
- Apple & Cinnamon Pie
- Black Bottom Cream Pie
- Raspberry & Coconut Pie
- Lemon Chiffon Pie
- Cherry Pie

CHAPTER FOUR

PIES & TARTS

Raisin Cheese Pie

Serves 8

½ cup, plus 1 tablespoon all-purpose flour, plus extra for dusting
½ cup self-rising flour
¾ stick (6 tablespoons) cold butter, diced
2 tablespoons cold water

For the filling
½ cup seedless raisins
2 tablespoons dark rum or orange juice
8 ounces ricotta cheese
2 eggs, separated
¼ cup granulated sugar
1 teaspoon pure vanilla extract
⅔ cup heavy cream

To decorate
Fresh mint leaves
Fresh raspberries

1 Sift the flours into a mixing bowl. Add the butter and rub it in until the mixture resembles bread crumbs. Sprinkle the water over the dry ingredients and mix to a firm dough. Knead briefly, then wrap in plastic wrap and chill for 30 minutes.

2 For the filling, put the raisins in a bowl with the rum or orange juice and set aside to soak.

3 Preheat the oven to 400°F. Roll out the dough on a lightly floured surface and use to line a 9-inch plain tart pan. Prick the base all over, then chill for 15 minutes.

4 Line the tart shell with parchment paper and baking beans. Blind bake for 10 minutes. Remove the paper and beans and bake for 5 minutes. Reduce the temperature to 300°F. Beat the cheese until soft, then stir in the raisins. Beat the egg yolks, sugar, and vanilla extract in another bowl until pale. Add the cream and continue beating until stiff. Fold into the raisin mixture.

5 Beat the egg whites in a clean bowl until stiff, then fold into the cheese mixture. Spoon into the pie shell and bake for 45–60 minutes, or until just set. Turn off the heat and cool in the oven for 15 minutes. Cool in the pan, then chill overnight. Decorate with mint leaves and raspberries.

Chess Pie

Serves 8

1⅓ cups all-purpose flour, plus extra
    for dusting
Pinch of salt
5 tablespoons cold butter, diced
2 tablespoons cold water
1–2 teaspoons confectioners' sugar,
    for dusting

For the filling
1 stick (8 tablespoons) butter, softened
1 cup, plus 2 tablespoons granulated
    sugar
Finely grated zest of ½ lemon
Pinch of salt
3 egg yolks
1 tablespoon lemon juice

1 Sift the flour and salt into a mixing bowl. Add the butter and rub it in until the mixture resembles bread crumbs. Sprinkle over the water and mix to a firm dough. Knead briefly, wrap in plastic wrap, and chill for 30 minutes.

2 Put a baking sheet in the oven and preheat to 400°F. Roll out the pastry on a floured surface and use to line a shallow 9-inch tart pan. Prick the base all over with a fork, then chill for 10 minutes.

3 Line the tart shell with parchment paper and fill with baking beans. Bake for 15 minutes. Remove the paper and beans, then bake for a further 5 minutes. Reduce the temperature to 325°F.

4 Cream the butter, sugar, lemon zest, and salt together in a bowl until light and fluffy. Beat in the egg yolks, one at a time, then stir in the lemon juice.

5 Spoon the filling into the tart shell and roughly spread it out. Bake for a further 25–30 minutes, or until lightly set.

6 Leave the pie to settle for 10 minutes before removing from the pan. Dust with confectioners' sugar before serving.

Coffee & Walnut Pie

Serves 4–6

1 cup, plus 2 tablespoons all-purpose
   flour, plus extra for dusting
Pinch of salt
²/₃ stick (5 tablespoons) cold butter,
   diced
2–3 tablespoons cold water
Whipped cream or ice cream, to serve

For the filling
¾ cup maple syrup
1 tablespoon instant coffee granules
1 tablespoon boiling water
¼ stick (2 tablespoons) butter, softened
²/₃ cup light brown sugar
3 eggs, beaten
1 teaspoon pure vanilla extract
½ cup walnut halves

1. Sift the flour and salt into a mixing bowl. Add the butter and rub it in until the mixture resembles fine bread crumbs. Add 2 tablespoons cold water and, using a spatula, start to bring the dough together, adding a little more water, if necessary. Knead briefly, then wrap in plastic wrap and chill for 20 minutes.

2. Roll out the dough on a lightly floured surface to a rough round at least 2 inches in diameter larger than a loose-bottomed 9-inch fluted tart pan. Gently roll the pastry on to the rolling pin, then unroll it over the pan to cover. Press the pastry into the edge of the pan, removing any overhanging pastry with a knife. Prick the base. Chill for 20 minutes.

3. Put a baking sheet in the oven and preheat to 400°F. Line the tart shell with parchment paper and fill with baking beans. Bake blind for 12 minutes. Remove the paper and beans and bake for a further 10 minutes, or until golden. Let cool. Reduce the oven temperature to 350°F.

4. For the filling, put the maple syrup in a saucepan and heat until almost boiling. Mix the coffee granules with the boiling water, stirring until they have completely dissolved. Stir this mixture into the maple syrup. Leave until just warm.

5. Combine the butter and sugar, and gradually beat in the eggs. Add the cooled maple syrup mixture with the vanilla extract, and stir well.

6. Arrange the walnut halves in the base of the tart shell, then carefully pour in the filling. Transfer to the oven and bake for 30–35 minutes, or until browned and firm. Let cool for about 10 minutes. Serve with whipped cream or ice cream.

Georgia Pecan Pie

Serves 8–10

1⅓ cups all-purpose flour, plus extra
   for dusting
⅓ cup cream cheese
1 stick (8 tablespoons) butter
2 tablespoons granulated sugar

For the filling
2½–3 cups pecan halves
3 eggs, lightly beaten
1 cup packed dark brown sugar
1½ cups light corn syrup
Grated zest and juice of ½ lemon
½ stick (4 tablespoons) butter, melted
   and cooled
2 teaspoons vanilla extract

Whipped cream or ice cream, to serve

1 Sift the flour into a mixing bowl. Add the cream cheese, butter, and sugar and rub it in until the mixture resembles fine bread crumbs. Form the dough into a ball, then flatten and wrap in plastic wrap. Chill 1 hour.

2 Roll the dough out on a lightly floured surface and carefully line the base and sides of a 9-inch tart pan. Crimp the edge and chill.

3 Preheat the oven to 350°F. Pick out ¾ cup perfect pecan halves and set aside. Coarsely chop the remaining nuts.

4 For the filling, whisk the eggs and brown sugar together in a bowl until light and foamy. Beat in the corn syrup, lemon zest and juice, melted butter, and vanilla extract. Stir in the chopped pecans and pour into the tart pan.

5 Set the pie on a baking sheet and carefully arrange the reserved pecan halves in concentric circles on top of the mixture.

6 Bake for 45 minutes until the filling has risen and set and the pecans have colored. Transfer to a wire rack to cool to room temperature. Serve with whipped cream or ice cream.

Freeform Strawberry &

Rhubarb Pie

Serves 4–6

1 cup all-purpose flour, plus extra for
    dusting
Pinch of salt
²⁄₃ stick (5 tablespoons) cold butter,
    diced
½ cup ground almonds
¼ cup granulated sugar
3–4 tablespoons cold water

For the filling
1 pound rhubarb, cut into chunks
⅓–½ cup granulated sugar, to taste
1 vanilla bean
2 strips lemon zest
2 teaspoons cornstarch or arrowroot
3 cups strawberries, hulled and
    halved if large
2 teaspoons coarse sugar

1 Sift the flour and salt into a mixing bowl. Add the butter and rub it in with the ground almonds and sugar until the mixture resembles coarse bread crumbs. Add enough cold water to form a dough. Knead briefly, then wrap in plastic wrap and chill for at least 20 minutes.

2 For the filling, put the rhubarb, ⅓ cup sugar, vanilla bean, and lemon zest into a saucepan over a low heat. Cook, stirring occasionally, for 8-10 minutes until the rhubarb is tender and quite juicy but still holding its shape. Taste for sweetness and add the remaining sugar if necessary.

3 Mix the cornstarch and a little water together until smooth. Stir into the rhubarb, then return to a gentle simmer. Cook for 1-2 minutes until thickened. Remove from the heat and stir in the strawberries. Let cool. Remove the vanilla bean and lemon zest.

4 Preheat the oven to 400°F. Roll the dough out on a lightly floured surface to a large round about 15 inches in diameter. Transfer to a large, nonstick baking sheet. Spoon the cold rhubarb mixture into the center of the dough and gather the dough around the filling, leaving an open top. Brush the dough with a little cold water and sprinkle with the coarse sugar.

5 Bake in the center of the oven for about 20-25 minutes. Let cool, then cut into wedges and serve.

Tip

A freeform pie is a great way to toss together something tasty when you don't have much time to make dessert. For fruit such as rhubarb, pears, and apples it's best to heat them over a low heat first to soften them up. With softer fruit such as nectarines, peaches, and bananas they will not need cooking as they will soften in the time it takes for the pie to bake. Just toss them with a little sugar.

Strawberry & Custard

Tartlets

Makes 2

¾ cup all-purpose flour, plus extra
   for dusting
3 tablespoons confectioners' sugar
¾ stick (6 tablespoons) butter
About 1 tablespoon water

For the filling
⅔ cup milk
1 egg yolk
2 tablespoons granulated sugar
2 tablespoons all-purpose flour

For the topping
6–8 strawberries, hulled
1 tablespoon strawberry jam

1 Sift the flour and confectioners' sugar into a mixing bowl. Add the butter and rub it in until the mixture resembles bread crumbs. Sprinkle over the water and mix to a firm dough. Knead briefly, wrap in plastic wrap, and chill for 30 minutes.

2 Roll out the dough on a lightly floured surface and use to line two 3-inch tartlet pans. Prick the bases all over with a fork and chill for 10 minutes.

3 Preheat the oven to 400°F. Line the tartlet shells with nonstick parchment paper and fill with baking beans. Bake for 15–20 minutes. Remove the paper and beans and bake for 5 minutes until pale golden. Let cool.

4 For the custard filling, beat the milk, egg yolk, sugar, and flour in a bowl. Pour into a small saucepan and cook, stirring continuously until the mixture comes to a boil. Beat the custard until smooth, then simmer for 2 minutes. Let cool, then spoon into the tartlet cases.

5 Arrange the strawberries on top of the custard. Warm the jam and brush it over the top. Let set for a few minutes before serving.

Peanut Butter Pie

Serves 8

3 eggs
1 cup light corn syrup
⅓ cup granulated sugar
½ cup creamy peanut butter
½ teaspoon pure vanilla extract
1 cup salted peanuts, coarsely chopped

For the topping
1½ cups heavy cream
2 tablespoons granulated sugar
½ teaspoon pure vanilla extract
1 x unbaked pie shell, never-fail or
   extra flaky

1 Chill the pie shell. Beat the eggs and add the corn syrup, sugar, peanut butter, and vanilla. Beat until smooth. Blend the salted peanuts into the mixture. Pour the filling into the chilled, unbaked pie shell and bake for 15 minutes at 400°F. Turn down the heat to 350°F and bake for an additional 30–35 minutes. Let cool.

2 Beat the heavy cream with the sugar and vanilla. Spread over the pie after it has cooled and serve.

Banana Tarte Tatin

Serves 4–6

½ stick (4 tablespoons) butter, plus
   extra for greasing
5 bananas
½ cup, plus 2 tablespoons sugar
2 tablespoons boiling water
2 pinches of ground cinnamon
8 ounces pastry dough, thawed if frozen
Flour, for dusting
Whipped cream, to serve

Tip

The riper the bananas
the better the taste.
Try not to buy ones that
are too ripe otherwise
the dessert may go
mushy.

1 Preheat the oven to 400°F. Grease a nonstick 9-inch cake pan.

2 Slice the bananas into ¼-inch rounds. Melt the butter with the sugar in a large skillet. Add the water and stir over a high heat until the sugar has dissolved and the water is a warm caramel color. Add the bananas to the skillet and cook for 1–2 minutes. Sprinkle the cinnamon over the bananas, then spoon them into the greased pan.

3 Roll the pastry out on a lightly floured surface to a round about 1 inch bigger than the cake pan. Drape it over the bananas and tuck the edges in. Bake for 20 minutes until the pastry is puffed and golden. Put a large serving plate over the pan and turn it upside down so the pastry is on the bottom. Remove the cake pan and leave for 5 minutes before serving with whipped cream.

Bourbon Pie

Serves 8–10

1⅓ cups all-purpose flour, plus extra
  for dusting
Pinch of salt
¾ stick (6 tablespoons) cold butter,
  diced
2 tablespoons cold water

For the filling
⅓ cup dark brown sugar
⅔ stick (5 tablespoons) butter, softened
3 eggs, lightly beaten
1 teaspoon cornstarch
⅔ cup light corn syrup
⅔ cup maple syrup
¼ cup bourbon
1 teaspoon pure vanilla extract
1½ cups chopped pecans or walnuts

For the bourbon cream
1 cup heavy cream
2 tablespoons bourbon
1 tablespoon dark brown sugar

1 Sift the flour and salt into a mixing bowl. Add the butter and rub it in until the mixture resembles bread crumbs. Sprinkle over the water and mix to a firm dough. Knead briefly, then wrap in plastic wrap and chill for 30 minutes.

2 Put a baking sheet in the oven and preheat to 400°F. Roll out the dough on a floured surface and use to line a 9-inch tart pan. Prick the base all over and chill for 10 minutes.

3 Line the tart shell with parchment paper and fill with baking beans. Bake for 15 minutes. Remove the paper and beans, brush the base with 1 teaspoon beaten egg from the filling and bake for 5 minutes. Reduce the oven temperature to 350°F.

4 Beat the sugar and butter until creamy. Gradually beat in the eggs and cornstarch. Stir in the syrups, bourbon, vanilla extract and nuts. Pour into the tart shell and bake for 35–40 minutes, or until the filling is just set.

5 For the cream, whip the cream, bourbon, and sugar together in a bowl until soft peaks form. Serve the pie warm with the cream.

Fig & Ricotta Tart

Serves 6–8

1⅓ cups all-purpose flour

⅔ cup ground rice

1¾ sticks (14 tablespoons) unsalted butter

½ cup granulated sugar

For the filling

16 ounces ricotta cheese

⅔ cup confectioners' sugar

2 teaspoons pure vanilla extract

6 ripe figs, quartered

2 tablespoons honey

1 Mix the flour and ground rice together. Cream the butter and sugar together in another bowl until light and fluffy. Mix in the flour and ground rice and bring together to form a ball.

2 Press the pastry into the base of a 9-inch loose-bottomed tart pan. Prick with a fork and chill for 20 minutes. Meanwhile, preheat the oven to 350°F.

3 Bake for 20–25 minutes. Let cool completely, then remove from the tart pan.

4 For the filling, beat the ricotta cheese, confectioners' sugar, and vanilla extract together in a bowl. Spread the mixture over the baked crust and arrange the figs over the ricotta. Drizzle with honey just before serving.

Tarte Fine aux Pommes

Serves 4–6

Butter, for greasing
12 ounces puff pastry dough,
  thawed if frozen
Flour, for dusting

For the filling
2 Golden Delicious apples
1½ tablespoons confectioners' sugar
2 tablespoons apricot jam
Light cream, to serve

Tip
Puff pastry has a high
fat content, which makes
it fragile compared
with other pastries so
try not to handle it
too much.

1 Preheat the oven to 375°F and lightly grease a baking sheet. Roll the pastry out thinly on a lightly floured surface and cut out a 9-inch round. Transfer to the prepared baking sheet.

2 Halve and core the apples and thinly slice lengthwise. Lay on the pastry in concentric circles, overlapping slightly and leaving a ½-inch margin around the edge. Dust with confectioners' sugar.

3 Transfer the baking sheet to the oven and bake for 20-25 minutes, or until the pastry is risen and golden and the apples are tender and golden at the edges.

4 Gently heat the apricot jam in a small saucepan, then press through a strainer to remove any large pieces. While the jam and tart are both hot, brush the jam generously over the apple slices. Let cool slightly and serve warm with cream.

Honey & Mixed Nut Tart

Serves 8

1½ cups all-purpose flour, plus extra
    for dusting
Pinch of salt
1 stick (8 tablespoons) cold butter,
    diced
2–3 tablespoons cold water
Heavy cream, to serve

For the filling
1 stick (8 tablespoons) butter
1 cup clear honey
2¼ cups mixed nuts, such as pecans,
    walnuts, hazelnuts, and almonds

1 Sift the flour and salt into a mixing bowl. Add the butter and rub it in until the mixture resembles fine bread crumbs. Add 2 tablespoons water and mix to a firm dough, adding more water, if needed. Knead briefly, then wrap in plastic wrap and chill for 20 minutes.

2 Roll out the dough on a floured surface to a rough round at least 2 inches larger than a loose-bottomed 9-inch fluted tart pan. Prick the base all over with a fork. Chill for 20 minutes.

3 Put a baking sheet in the oven and preheat to 400°F. Line the tart shell with parchment paper and fill with baking beans. Bake blind for 12 minutes, then remove the paper and beans and bake for 10 minutes, or until pale golden. Cool on a wire rack. Reduce the oven temperature to 375°F.

4 Heat the butter and honey gently until melted, then increase the heat and let bubble for 1–2 minutes, or until starting to darken. Stir in the nuts and return to simmering point. Cool slightly.

5 Pour the filling into the tart shell and bake for 5-7 minutes, or until the nuts are golden and the crust is browned. Serve warm with cream.

Orange Chiffon Pie

Serves 6-8

18–20 graham crackers, finely crushed
⅓ stick (3 tablespoons) butter, melted
2 tablespoons granulated sugar
  (optional)
Whipped cream, to serve

For the filling
¼ cup cold water
1 packet powdered gelatin
4 eggs, separated
1⅓ cups granulated sugar
Grated zest of 1 orange
½ cup freshly squeezed orange juice
¼ teaspoon cream of tartar

To decorate
Julienne strips of orange zest
  simmered in water until tender

1 Combine the graham cracker crumbs, melted butter, and sugar, if using, in a large bowl. Pour into a 9-inch pie pan and, using an 8-inch pie pan, press the crumbs firmly against the base and sides of the larger pan. Alternatively, use the back of a tablespoon to press the crumbs against the base and sides of the pan. Chill until firm.

2 For the filling, pour the water into a coffee cup or a small bowl, sprinkle over the gelatin and let stand for 10 minutes. Set the cup in a saucepan of simmering water and heat gently for 5 minutes, stirring, until the gelatin has dissolved.

3 Using an electric mixer, beat the egg yolks in a large heatproof bowl for 1–2 minutes until light and fluffy. Gradually beat in half the sugar, the grated orange zest, and juice. Set the bowl over a saucepan of simmering water (the base of the bowl should just touch the water) and cook, stirring, for about 8–10 minutes, until the mixture thickens and coats the back of a wooden spoon. Remove the bowl from the water, stir in the gelatin mixture, and cool the custard, stirring occasionally.

4 Using clean beaters, beat the egg whites and cream of tartar in a large clean bowl until fluffy. Increase the speed and beat until soft peaks form. Gradually whisk in the remaining sugar until the whites are stiff and glossy.

5 Beat a spoonful of the whites into the custard, then pour the mixture over the whites and fold together until just blended. Pour into the pan, mounding the mixture in the middle, and chill for 4–6 hours until set. Decorate with orange zest and serve with whipped cream.

Banana Cream Pie

Serves 8

2 cups vanilla wafer crumbs
4 tablespoons butter, melted

For the filling
⅓ cup cornstarch
½ cup granulated sugar
2 cups milk
1 cup light cream
¼ stick (2 tablespoons) butter
3 egg yolks
½ teaspoon pure vanilla extract
3 medium bananas
2 tablespoons orange juice

For the topping
⅔ cup heavy cream
1 tablespoon confectioners' sugar, sifted
½ teaspoon pure vanilla extract

1 Mix the wafer crumbs and melted butter together, and press the mixture evenly over the base and up the sides of a 8–9-inch pie dish. Chill while making the filling.

2 For the filling, blend the cornstarch, sugar, and a little of the milk into a paste in a saucepan, then stir in the remaining milk and cream. Add the butter and cook over a low heat, stirring continuously, until the mixture boils and thickens. Simmer for a further 1 minute.

3 Remove the pan from the heat and let cool for 1 minute. Mix the egg yolks in a bowl, then stir in a large spoonful of the custard mixture. Stir the egg mixture into the custard mixture, then stir in the vanilla extract. Return to a very low heat and cook for about 5 minutes until the mixture has thickened slightly. Do not let the custard boil or it may curdle.

4 Slice 2 bananas and toss in the orange juice. Remove them from the juice, reserving the juice, and use to cover the base of the pie shell. Pour the custard over the bananas. Let cool, then chill for 2 hours.

5 For the topping, whip the cream, confectioners' sugar, and vanilla extract until soft peaks form. Spoon and spread the cream in the center of the pie, leaving a border of custard showing.

6 Slice the remaining banana and toss in the orange juice. Arrange in an overlapping circle on top of the cream and serve at once.

Marlborough Pie

Serves 8

1⅓ cups all-purpose flour, plus extra
   for dusting
½ teaspoon ground cinnamon
2 tablespoons granulated sugar
1 stick (8 tablespoons) cold butter,
   diced
1 egg yolk
2–3 teaspoons cold water

For the filling
12 ounces tart apples, peeled, cored,
   and roughly chopped
¼ stick (2 tablespoons) butter
1 tablespoon lemon juice and finely
   grated zest of ½ a small lemon
¼ cup light brown sugar
½ cup heavy cream
2 egg yolks
⅓ cup raisins
½ cup chopped toasted walnuts or
   pecans

For the meringue topping
3 egg whites
1½ cups confectioners' sugar, sifted
½ teaspoon vanilla extract

1 Sift the flour and cinnamon into a bowl. Stir in the sugar. Add the butter and rub it in until the mixture resembles bread crumbs. Mix the egg yolk with 2 teaspoons water and sprinkle over the dry ingredients. Mix to a firm dough, adding extra water if needed. Knead, wrap, and chill for 30 minutes.

2 Put a baking sheet in the oven and preheat to 400°F. Roll out the dough and use to line a 9-inch tart pan. Prick the base and chill for 10 minutes. Line the pie shell with parchment paper and fill with baking beans. Bake blind for 15 minutes. Remove the paper and beans and bake for 5 minutes. Let cool. Reduce the oven temperature to 325°F.

3 Heat the apples, butter, and lemon juice gently until tender and pulpy. Press through a strainer into a bowl. Add the lemon zest and sugar and stir until dissolved. Mix in the cream, then the egg yolks. For the topping, beat the egg whites until peaks form, then set over a pan of simmering water. Add the sugar and vanilla. Beat until thick. Remove from the heat and beat for 2 minutes.

4 Spread the raisins and nuts in the pie, then pour in the apple filling. Spread the meringue on top. Bake for 30 minutes, or until the meringue is dark golden and crisp.

Freeform Spiced Plum Pie

Serves 6–8

½ cup pecans, very finely chopped
1½ cups all-purpose flour
1¼ sticks (10 tablespoons) unsalted
 butter, diced
½ cup sour cream
Whipped cream, to serve

For the filling
2 pounds ripe plums, pitted and
 quartered
½ cup packed light brown sugar
1 teaspoon ground cinnamon
½ teaspoon ground ginger
Pinch of freshly grated nutmeg

Tip
Always flour the work
surface and rolling pin lightly
before rolling out the dough to
prevent it sticking. You can always
sprinkle extra flour onto the
rolling pin or work surface
if it is starting to stick.

1 Put the pecans, flour, and butter in a food processor and process briefly until the mixture forms very coarse bread crumbs. Add the sour cream and process for a further 4–5 seconds. Alternatively, rub the butter into the flour using your hands or a pastry cutter and mix in the cream.

2 Turn the dough out on to a lightly floured board and bring the mixture together with your hands. Wrap in plastic wrap and let chill for 20 minutes.

3 For the filling, put the plums in a bowl and mix with the brown sugar and spices.

4 Roll out the dough on a lightly floured surface into a round 14-inches in diameter, and put on a nonstick baking sheet. Pile the plums into the center of the pastry, leaving a 3-inch margin.

5 Bring up the sides of the dough to half-cover the plums, then chill the pie for 20 minutes. Preheat the oven to 400°F, then bake for 40–45 minutes. Serve with whipped cream.

Caramel Cream Pie

Serves 8

1⅓ cups all-purpose flour, plus extra
   for dusting
Pinch of salt
⅔ stick (5 tablespoons) cold butter, diced
2–3 tablespoons water

For the filling
2 eggs, lightly beaten
½ cup granulated sugar
⅓ cup hot water
1¾ cups milk
⅓ stick (3 tablespoons) butter
⅓ cup all-purpose flour
¾ cup light brown sugar
3 tablespoons heavy cream

For the topping
1 cup heavy cream
1 tablespoon light brown sugar
Pinch of cream of tartar

1 Sift the flour and salt into a mixing bowl. Add the butter and rub it in until the mixture resembles fine bread crumbs. Sprinkle over the water and mix to a firm dough, adding a little extra water if necessary. Knead briefly, then wrap in plastic wrap and chill for 30 minutes.

2 Put a baking sheet in the oven and preheat to 400°F. Roll out the dough on a lightly floured surface and use to line a 9-inch tart pan. Prick the base and chill for 10 minutes.

3 Line the tart shell with parchment paper and fill with baking beans. Bake blind for 15 minutes. Remove the paper and beans, brush the base with 1 teaspoon beaten egg from the filling, and bake for 5 minutes. Reduce the oven temperature to 325°F.

4 Put the sugar and 2 tablespoons water in a saucepan over a low heat. When the sugar has dissolved, increase the heat and cook, without stirring, until it is dark golden. Remove from the heat and carefully pour in the hot water. Cool slightly, then stir in the milk. Melt the butter in another pan, then remove from the heat and stir in the flour and brown sugar. Stir in the eggs, then the caramel mixture and cream. Cook over a low heat, stirring, until the mixture thickens, but do not boil.

5 Pour the filling into the tart shell and bake for 20 minutes, or until lightly set. Leave on a wire rack until cold. Chill for 2 hours. Pour the cream into a chilled bowl and stir in the sugar and cream of tartar. Whip until soft peaks form, then spread over the filling.

Blacksmith Pie

Serves 6–8

²/₃ stick (5 tablespoons) butter
10–12 chocolate-covered graham
   crackers, crushed
1 teaspoon cocoa powder

For the filling
3 tablespoons cornstarch
1 cup granulated sugar, plus
   2 tablespoons
1 cup milk
½ cup light cream
2 egg yolks
1 egg
½ cup chocolate chips
1¼ cups heavy cream
1 teaspoon pure vanilla extract
2 egg whites

1 Line the base of an 8–9-inch round loose-bottomed pan with parchment paper. Melt the butter in a saucepan, then stir in the cracker crumbs and mix together. Press over the base and sides of the pan. Chill while making the filling.

2 Combine the cornstarch, the 2 tablespoons sugar, milk and light cream in a saucepan.

Stir over a low heat with a whisk until thickened and smooth. Turn off the heat.

3 Beat the egg yolks and egg together. Stir in a spoonful of hot custard, then stir the egg mixture into the rest of the custard in the pan. Slowly bring to a boil, stirring, until slightly thickened.

4 Transfer 1 cup of the hot custard to a bowl. Add the chocolate chips and stir until melted. Spoon into the pie shell, spreading over the base and slightly up the sides. Chill.

5 Cover the remaining custard with dampened parchment paper and let cool. Beat the heavy cream, vanilla extract, and half the sugar until soft peaks form. Beat the egg whites in a clean, grease-free bowl until stiff, then gradually beat in the remaining sugar.

6 Stir the custard until smooth. Fold in the whipped cream and meringue mixture. Pour into the pie shell and chill for at least 1 hour. Dust with the cocoa powder before serving.

Pear Tart with Walnut
& Star Anise

Serves 6

1¾ cups all-purpose flour
Pinch of salt
2 egg yolks
1 stick (8 tablespoons) butter, plus
   extra for greasing
3 tablespoons granulated sugar
Beaten egg, for glazing

For the filling
¾ cup granulated sugar
1¾ cups water
6 whole star anise
7 small, firm, just-ripe pears
2 tablespoons lemon juice
1 egg, beaten
6 whole cloves
Large strip pared lemon zest, cut into
   fine shreds
About 12 walnut halves

1 Sift the flour and salt on to a work surface. Make a well in the center. Add the egg yolks, butter, and sugar and work these together. Gradually work in the flour. Knead, then wrap and chill for 1 hour.

2 Put the sugar, water, and 2 star anise in a saucepan. Heat until the sugar dissolves, then bring to a boil and simmer for 1 minute. Halve and peel the pears. Scoop out the core, then brush each half with lemon juice. Add to the syrup, cover and leave to simmer for 20 minutes, or until tender, turning occasionally.

3 Preheat the oven to 375°F and grease a baking sheet. Roll out the dough on a lightly floured surface and cut out a 10-inch round. Put on a baking sheet and push the edge of the dough in slightly to form a thicker pie edge. Prick the base all over. Re-roll the dough trimmings and cut out star shapes with a small cutter. Arrange around the edge, attaching with beaten egg. Brush with beaten egg, then bake for 12–15 minutes.

4 Arrange the cooked pears cut-side up in the tart shell. Add the remaining star anise, cloves, zest, and walnuts to the syrup. Bring to a rapid boil for 5 minutes, until thickened. Strain the syrup, reserve and scatter the star anise, zest and walnuts on top of the pears. Drizzle over a little syrup and serve hot.

Chocolate Chip
& Peanut Butter Pie

Serves 8

1⅓ cups all-purpose flour, plus extra
   for dusting
Pinch of salt
³/₄ stick (6 tablespoons) cold butter,
   diced
2 tablespoons cold water

For the filling
3 eggs, lightly beaten
½ cup smooth peanut butter
½ cup packed brown sugar
¾ cup light corn syrup
1 teaspoon pure vanilla extract
⅔ cup plain chocolate chips

1 Sift the flour and salt into a mixing bowl. Add the butter and rub it in until the mixture resembles fine bread crumbs. Sprinkle over the water and mix to a firm dough. Knead briefly, then wrap in plastic wrap and chill for 30 minutes.

2 Roll out the pastry on a lightly floured surface and use to line a shallow 9-inch pie dish. Prick the base all over with a fork, then crimp the edge or decorate with the fork. Chill for 10 minutes.

3 Put a baking sheet in the oven and preheat to 400°F. Line the pie shell with parchment paper and fill with baking beans. Bake for 15 minutes. Remove the paper and beans, brush the base with 1 teaspoon beaten egg from the filling, and bake for a further 5 minutes. Reduce the oven temperature to 350°F.

4 For the filling, combine the peanut butter, sugar, syrup, eggs, and vanilla extract in a bowl. Stir in the chocolate chips. Pour the filling into the pie shell and bake for 30 minutes. The center will still be slightly wobbly, but will firm up as it cools.

5 Remove from the oven and let stand for 15 minutes on a wire rack, then remove the pie from the pan and cool before serving.

Frangipani Cream Pie

Serves 8

6½ ounces puff pastry dough, thawed if
  frozen
Flour, for dusting
1 cup ground almonds
½ cup, plus 2 tablespoons caster sugar
⅓ stick (3 tablespoons) butter, softened
3 eggs, lightly beaten
1 tablespoon all-purpose flour
3 tablespoons apricot jam

For the topping
⅔ cup heavy cream
2 tablespoons confectioners' sugar,
  sifted
2 drops pure almond extract

1 Roll out the dough on a lightly floured surface, and use to line a 10-inch pie dish. Prick the base all over with a fork and crimp the edge of the pastry with the back of a knife. Chill in the refrigerator while making the filling.

2 Put a baking sheet in the oven and preheat to 400°F. Put the almonds, sugar, and butter in a bowl and beat together. Gradually beat in the eggs a little at a time. Sift over the flour and stir in, together with 1 tablespoon of the cream from the topping.

3 Spread the jam over the base of the pie shell, then spoon the filling over the jam and spread it out evenly. Bake for 30 minutes, or until the filling is set and the crust is browned and crisp.

4 Chill the pie in the refrigerator for 1 hour. For the topping, pour the cream into a chilled bowl and stir in 1 tablespoon of the confectioners' sugar and the almond extract. Whip until soft peaks form, then spoon into a piping bag and pipe swirls of cream around the edge of the pie. Dust with the remaining confectioners' sugar before serving.

Figgy Meringue Tarts

Makes 4

2 egg whites

½ cup, plus 2 tablespoons granulated
  sugar

4 prepared single-serving graham
  cracker crusts

4 ripe figs

For the filling

1⅓ cups milk

2 egg yolks

4 tablespoons granulated sugar

4 tablespoons all-purpose flour

Tip

When buying figs,
always look for ones that
are soft and have a sweet
aroma. Avoid any that
look too soft.

1. Preheat the oven to 425°F. For the custard filling, beat the milk, egg yolk, sugar, and flour in a bowl. Pour into a small saucepan and cook, stirring continuously until the mixture comes to a boil. Beat the custard until smooth, then simmer for 2 minutes. Let cool, then spoon into the tartlet cases.

2. Whisk the egg whites in a clean, grease-free bowl until stiff. Gradually whisk in the sugar a little at a time, whisking well between each addition until the mixture is thick and glossy.

3. Arrange the custard tarts on a baking sheet and bake for 6–8 minutes until warmed through. Remove from the oven and top each with a fig.

4. Spoon the meringue mixture evenly over each fig to cover them completely. Using the tip of a knife to gently pull the meringue into peaks. Bake for 4–5 minutes until lightly golden and just warm.

Apple & Cinnamon Pie

Serves 6–8

1¾ cups all-purpose flour, plus extra
    for dusting
Pinch of salt
1 stick (8 tablespoons) cold unsalted
    butter, diced
¼ cup granulated sugar
2–3 tablespoons cold water
Milk, for brushing

For the filling
¼–⅓ cup granulated sugar, plus extra
    for sprinkling
1 teaspoon ground cinnamon
2¼ pounds Golden Delicious apples,
    peeled, cored and thinly sliced

1 Sift the flour and salt into a mixing bowl. Add the butter and rub it in until the mixture resembles bread crumbs. Add the sugar, then sprinkle over the water and mix to a firm dough. Knead, wrap in plastic wrap, and chill for 30 minutes.

2 Preheat the oven to 400°F. Divide the dough into 2 pieces. Roll out one piece on a lightly floured surface into a 10-inch diameter round and use to line a 9-inch pie pan.

3 Mix the sugar and cinnamon together in a bowl and sprinkle over the sliced apples. Arrange the apple slices in the pan—don't worry if the apples are above the top of the pan.

4 Roll out the remaining pastry into a 10-inch diameter round. Brush the edge of the dough in the pan with a little milk. Carefully lay the dough over the apples and press down the edges to seal. Trim off any excess dough and decorate the edge with a fork, if liked. Make 2 slashes in the top of the pie, or prick with a fork a couple of times.

5 Brush the top of the dough with a little milk, then sprinkle with sugar. Bake in the center of the oven for 25–30 minutes until the crust is golden and the apples are tender. Serve warm or cold.

Black Bottom Cream Pie

Serves 8

¾ cup, plus 2 tablespoons all-purpose
    flour
3 tablespoons cocoa powder
2 tablespoons confectioners' sugar
⅔ stick (5 tablespoons) cold butter,
    diced
1 egg yolk
1 tablespoon cold water
Grated chocolate, to decorate

For the filling
4 egg yolks
¼ cup granulated sugar
4 teaspoons cornstarch
1¾ cups milk
2 ounces semisweet chocolate
1 tablespoon dark rum

For the topping
1½ teaspoons powdered gelatin
2 tablespoons cold water
½ cup heavy cream
2 tablespoons dark rum
3 egg whites
⅓ cup confectioners' sugar, sifted
½ teaspoon cream of tartar

1 Sift the flour, cocoa, and confectioners' sugar into a bowl. Add the butter and rub it in until the mixture resembles bread crumbs. Mix the egg yolk and water, add to the dry ingredients and mix to a firm dough. Knead, wrap, and chill for 30 minutes.

2 Put a baking sheet in the oven and preheat to 400°F. Grease a 9-inch pie pan. Roll out the dough and use to line the pan. Prick the base, line with foil and fill with baking beans. Bake for 15 minutes. Remove the foil and beans and bake for a further 10 minutes. Let cool.

3 Beat the egg yolks, granulated sugar, and cornstarch together. Bring the milk to a boil, then pour over the egg mixture, beating. Return to a low heat and stir until thick. Remove from the heat and stir in the chocolate until melted, then the rum. Spoon into the case and cool. Sprinkle the gelatin over the water and soak for 5 minutes. Set the bowl over a pan of simmering water and stir until dissolved. Cool slightly. Whip the cream until soft peaks form, then beat in the gelatin and rum. Chill for 30 minutes.

4 Beat the egg whites until stiff, then beat in the confectioners' sugar, a tablespoon at a time, with the cream of tartar. Fold into the cream mixture, then spoon on top of the pie. Chill until set, then decorate with grated chocolate.

Raspberry & Coconut Pie

Serves 8

2 cups all-purpose flour, plus extra
  for dusting
Pinch of salt
$2/3$ stick (5 tablespoons) cold butter, diced
$1/4$ cup shortening
2–3 tablespoons cold water

For the filling
$1\frac{1}{2}$ sticks (12 tablespoons) butter
1 cup granulated sugar
3 eggs, beaten
$2\frac{1}{4}$ cups dried coconut
$1/4$ cup raspberry jam

Tip
When lining the tart pan
with the pastry dough, ease the
pastry carefully into the pan. Do
not pull or stretch the dough,
otherwise it may tear. It if does,
just moisten the edges with a
little water and gently
press together.

1 Sift the flour and salt into a mixing bowl. Add the butter and shortening and rub it in until the mixture resembles fine bread crumbs. Add 2 tablespoons water and mix to a firm dough, adding a little more water, if necessary. Knead briefly, then wrap in plastic wrap and chill for 20 minutes.

2 Roll out the dough on a lightly floured surface and use to line a rectangular 12 x 8-inch loose-bottomed tart pan. Prick the base with a fork and chill for 10 minutes.

3 Put a baking sheet in the oven and preheat to 375°F.

4 For the filling, beat the butter and sugar together in a bowl until light and fluffy. Slowly beat in the eggs, then fold in the dry coconut.

5 Spread the jam over the pastry base and spoon the coconut mixture on top, levelling out the surface. Bake for 35–40 minutes. Let cool a little, then cut into slices.

Lemon Chiffon Pie

Serves 6–8

1⅓ cups all-purpose flour, plus extra
   for dusting
Pinch of salt
¾ stick (6 tablespoons) butter, diced
¼ cup granulated sugar
2 teaspoons grated lemon zest
2 tablespoons cold water
1 egg yolk

For the filling
1 cup granulated sugar
3 eggs
Grated zest and juice of 3 large lemons
⅔ stick (5 tablespoons) butter
2 egg whites

1 Sift the flour and salt into a mixing bowl. Add the butter and rub it in until the mixture resembles bread crumbs. Stir in the sugar and lemon zest. Mix the water and egg yolk together and add to the bowl. Mix to a firm dough. Knead, wrap, and chill for 30 minutes.

2 Preheat the oven to 400°F. Roll out the dough on a lightly floured surface and use to line a 9-inch tart pan. Prick the base all over, then chill for 15 minutes. Line the tart shell with parchment paper and fill with baking beans. Blind bake for 10 minutes. Remove the paper and beans and bake for 5 minutes. Reduce the oven temperature to 300°F.

3 Whisk half the sugar, the eggs, the lemon zest and juice, and butter together in a heatproof bowl. Put the bowl over a saucepan of simmering water and whisk for 15 minutes until thick. Put the base of the bowl into cold water. Whisk until cool. Beat the egg whites in a clean bowl until stiff, then gradually beat in the remaining sugar until thick and shiny. Fold a large spoonful of the mixture into the lemon mixture, then fold in the remaining egg whites. Pour into the pie shell.

4 Bake in the center of the oven for 25–30 minutes until just set. Cool before serving.

Cherry Pie

Serves 6–8

3 cups all-purpose flour, plus extra
for dusting

½ teaspoon salt

1 stick (8 tablespoons) unsalted butter,
diced

½ cup shortening

2–3 tablespoons cold water

Milk, for brushing

For the filling

1¾ pounds fresh or canned cherries,
pitted

¼ cup granulated sugar, plus extra for
sprinkling

2 teaspoons cornstarch

½ teaspoon ground cinnamon

Pinch of freshly grated nutmeg

1 Sift the flour and salt into a mixing bowl. Add the butter and fat and rub it in until the mixture resembles fine bread crumbs. Add 2 tablespoons water and mix to a firm dough, adding more water, if necessary. Knead briefly, then wrap in plastic wrap and chill for 20 minutes.

2 Preheat the oven to 400°F. For the filling, mix the cherries, sugar, cornstarch, and spices together in a bowl.

3 Divide the dough into 2 pieces, one a little larger than the other. Roll out the larger piece of pastry on a lightly floured surface and use to line an 8-inch deep-dish pie pan. Spoon the filling into the pan. Brush the edges of the dough with milk.

4 Roll out the remaining dough and use to make a lid, pressing the edges together to seal. Trim the excess dough and crimp or score the edges. Score the surface of the pie to decorate. Chill for 20 minutes, then brush the top with extra milk and sprinkle with sugar.

5 Bake for 45 minutes, or until golden. Let stand for 5 minutes before serving.

FRUITY FAVORITES

- Apricot & Banana Crumble
- Apple & Raisin Crumble
- Fruity Meringue Crush
- Strawberry Cheesecake
- Peach, Pecan & Caramel Waffles
- Summer Berry Crêpes
- Blueberry & White Chocolate Meringue Roll
- Upside-down Pear Tart with Cardamom
- Rhubarb, Orange & Ginger Fool
- Berry Shortcake
- Candied Fruit Bombe
- Fried Bananas with Rum & Brown Sugar
- Cherry Syllabub
- Prunes Steeped in Tea with Vanilla

- Sweet & Nutty Caramel Strawberries
- Pineapple Upside-down Cake
- Summer Berry Galette
- Muscat-poached Grapes with Thick Creamy Yogurt
- Spiced Baked Apples
- Strawberries in Pimm's Syrup with Shortbread
- Orange Terrine with Citrus Cream
- Fresh Figs Baked
- Raspberry Surprise
- Tropical Fruit Salad
- Black Currant Pudding
- Tarte Tatin
- Berry Cornmeal Cake
- Seared Fruit in Frothy Orange Sauce
- Gooseberry Pie
- Pavlova with Tropical Fruits

CHAPTER FIVE

FRUITY
FAVORITES

Apricot & Banana Crumble

Serves 4-6

2 cups dried apricots
1 cup fresh orange juice
4 bananas
¼ teaspoon ground cinnamon
¼ teaspoon ground ginger
Light cream, to serve

For the topping
1½ cups all-purpose flour
½ cup packed light brown sugar
1 stick (8 tablespoons) unsalted butter

1 Soak the apricots in the orange juice for 2 hours until they have plumped up.

2 Preheat the oven to 400°F. Carefully slice the bananas into ½-inch rounds and mix with the apricots and spices. Put in an ovenproof dish.

3 For the topping, mix the flour and brown sugar together in a bowl. Add the butter and rub it in until it forms coarse bread crumbs. Sprinkle the mixture over the fruit.

4 Cook in the oven for 35-40 minutes until golden. Serve warm with cream.

Tip
For a crunchier topping, add ⅓ cup each of rolled oats and chopped hazelnuts to the crumble mix in step 3.

Apple & Raisin Crumble

Serves 4

1⅓ cups all-purpose flour
Pinch of salt
1 stick (8 tablespoons) unsalted butter, diced
⅓ cup old-fashioned rolled oats
⅓ cup packed light brown sugar
2¼ pounds Golden Delicious apples
⅓ cup raisins
Light cream, to serve

1 Preheat the oven to 400°F. Put the flour and salt in a mixing bowl. Add the butter and rub it in until the mixture resembles coarse bread crumbs—a few large lumps of butter are fine.

2 Stir in the oats and sugar. Peel the apples, quarter lengthwise and core them. Slice the apples very thinly and put them into an ovenproof dish. Scatter over the raisins. Spoon over the flour mixture to cover the fruit evenly. Transfer to the oven and bake for 25–30 minutes. Serve warm or cold with cream.

Tip

Crumbles are a good all-round family sweet dish, which can be varied not just by using fruits in season, but also by ringing the changes with the crumble topping. Whatever problems you may have with your pastry-making technique, you're absolutely safe with a crumble because there is no resting or roll-out involved.

Fruity Meringue Crush

Serves 2

2 store-bought meringue nests

⅔ cup Greek yogurt

5 strawberries, hulled and halved, plus extra to decorate

1 Roughly crush the meringue nests and reserve on a plate. Put the yogurt in a bowl and gently fold in the crushed meringue nests and strawberries.

2 Scatter a few extra strawberries on top to decorate and serve immediately with 2 spoons.

Tip

You can make this fabulous dessert using other fruits too. Try it with raspberries or sliced peaches in place of the strawberries, if you prefer.

Strawberry Cheesecake

Serves 10–12

For the crust
Sunflower oil, for oiling
2⅓ cups graham crackers, finely crushed
⅓ stick (3 tablespoons) butter, melted
¼ cup candied peel, very finely chopped (optional)

For the filling
20 ounces full-fat cream cheese
¾ cup, plus 2 tablespoons sugar
1 teaspoon pure vanilla extract
1⅓ cups whipping cream, whipped to soft peaks

For the topping
2 pints strawberries, hulled
2–3 tablespoons confectioners' sugar, to taste
Juice of ½ lemon

1 For the crust, lightly oil an 8-inch springform cake pan. Mix the cracker crumbs with the melted butter and candied peel, if using. Spread in an even layer over the base of the pan and press down well. Chill while you make the filling.

2 For the filling, beat the cheese, sugar, and vanilla extract together until smooth. Carefully fold in the whipped cream, taking care not to overbeat or the mixture will separate. Spread this mixture on top of the crust and level the surface. Chill for at least 4 hours, or preferably overnight.

3 For the topping, put 1 cup of the strawberries, confectioners' sugar and lemon juice in a food processor and process to a purée. Press through a sieve to remove the seeds. Halve the remaining strawberries and put into a bowl with the puréed strawberries. Mix together. Taste and add more strawberries. Mix together, then taste and add more confectioners' sugar if necessary.

4 To serve, loosen the pan and remove the outer ring and put on to a large serving plate. Spoon the strawberry purée over the top, allowing a little to run down the sides. Top with the remaining strawberries and cut into small wedges (it's very rich) and serve.

Peach, Pecan & Caramel

Waffles

Makes 8–10 waffles

1¾ cups all-purpose flour
2 teaspoons baking powder
1 teaspoon baking soda
2 eggs
⅓ stick (3 tablespoons) melted butter
¾ cup milk
1¼ cups buttermilk
1 teaspoon pure vanilla extract

To serve
2 peaches
⅔ cup pecans, chopped
1 tablespoon light brown sugar
5 tablespoons maple syrup
3 tablespoons dark rum

1 For the waffles, sift the dry ingredients into a large bowl. Whisk in the eggs, butter, and milk, gradually incorporating the flour until smooth.

2 Add the buttermilk and vanilla extract to the mixture. Cover and let stand for 30 minutes. Heat a stove-top or electric waffle iron and pour a ladleful over two-thirds of the iron. Close it and wipe off any excess batter.

3 Cook for 3–4 minutes, following the manufacturer's instructions.

4 When the batter stops steaming, open the iron and lift out the waffle with a fork. Keep hot in the oven.

5 Preheat the broiler. Slice the peaches into wedges and spread over a baking sheet. Scatter the pecans over the top, then sprinkle over the brown sugar. Drizzle with the maple syrup and dark rum and cook under the hot broiler until the sugar is bubbling and the pecans are golden.

6 Spoon the peaches and pecans on top of the waffles and drizzle over some of the juices.

Summer Berry Crêpes

Serves 4

¾ cup all-purpose flour
Pinch of salt
1 large egg
1¼ cups milk
A few drops of vanilla extract
¼ cup water
1 tablespoon butter
1 tablespoon sunflower oil
Whipped cream, to serve

For the fruit
1 tablespoon butter
¼ cup granulated sugar
1 teaspoon grated orange zest
5 tablespoons fresh orange juice
3 cups mixed summer fruits, such as
    strawberries, raspberries,
    blueberries
2 tablespoons white rum

To decorate
Fresh fruit or mint leaves
Strips of orange zest

1 Sift the flour and salt into a mixing bowl and make a well in the center. Break in the egg and gradually add half the milk, whisking briskly to draw the flour into the egg.

2 Whisk in the remaining milk, vanilla extract, and the water to make a smooth batter which has the consistency of single cream.

3 Heat a small skillet and add the butter and oil. When the butter has melted, pour into a small bowl and return the pan to the heat. Add a small ladleful of the batter mixture and swirl around the base of the pan until evenly coated. Cook until golden, then flip over and cook on the other side, 1-2 minutes in total. Slide the crêpe on to a plate. Repeat with the remaining batter, adding a little of the butter and oil mixture between crêpes.

4 For the fruit, melt the butter in a saucepan, stir in the sugar, and cook gently for 1-2 minutes until golden brown. Add the orange zest and juice and swirl the pan until the sugar has dissolved. Add the fruit and rum and cook until the fruit juices begin to run. Fold 2 crêpes on to each serving plate and top with a spoonful of the fruit. Decorate with fresh fruit or mint and strips of orange zest and serve with cream, if liked.

Blueberry & White
Chocolate Meringue Roll

Serves 6

⅓ cup granulated sugar
½ vanilla bean
5 egg whites
Confectioners' sugar for dusting

For the filling
5 ounces white chocolate
½ cup plain yogurt
1 cup mascarpone cheese
1 cup blueberries

1 Preheat the oven to 425°F. Grease and line with parchment paper a 9 x 13-inch baking sheet with sides.

2 Combine the confectioners' sugar and the seeds from inside the vanilla bean. Whisk the egg whites in a clean, grease-free bowl until stiff. Gradually whisk in the vanilla sugar a spoonful at a time until it forms a stiff, glossy meringue.

3 Spread the meringue mixture into the prepared pan and bake for 8 minutes. Reduce the oven temperature to 325°F and continue cooking for 10 minutes, or until firm to the touch.

4 Remove the meringue from the oven and turn out on to a sheet of parchment paper dusted with confectioners' sugar. Peel off the lining paper from the base and let cool for 10 minutes.

5 Meanwhile, for the filling, melt the chocolate in a bowl set over a saucepan of simmering water. Stir in the yogurt, then beat into the mascarpone. Spread the this mixture over the meringue and top with the blueberries. Roll up from one of the long sides using the paper underneath to help. Leave wrapped in the paper for at least 1 hour before serving, dusted with confectioners' sugar.

Upside-down Pear Tart

with Cardamom

Serves 4–6

1 cup, plus 2 tablespoons granulated
   sugar
3–4 tablespoons cold water
About 10 green cardamom pods
4–6 ripe but firm pears, depending on
   size, cored and quartered lengthwise
⅓ stick (3 tablespoons) unsalted butter,
   diced
16 ounces puff pastry dough, thawed if
   frozen
Flour, for dusting
Crème fraîche or sour cream to serve

1 Put the sugar and water into a 10-inch
   ovenproof skillet. Stir over a low heat until the
sugar has dissolved completely. Increase the heat
and bring the mixture to a rapid simmer.

2 Remove the seeds from the cardamoms and
   finely crush. As soon as the sugar begins to
color, sprinkle over the cardamom seeds. Do not
stir. Carefully add the pear quarters in concentric
circles. The sugar will slow down, but you must
watch it now as you want it to color evenly. Tilt and
turn the pan often until the sugar bubbling up
between the pears is deep brown and smells nutty.
Immediately remove from the heat and add butter
wherever there are spaces between the fruit. Let
cool for about 20 minutes.

3 Preheat the oven to 400°F. Roll out the puff
   pastry dough thinly on a lightly floured surface,
then cut a round about 1-inch larger than the
diameter of the skillet. Carefully put the pastry over
the pears, tucking it down the sides of the pan to
enclose the fruit.

4 Transfer the skillet to the oven and bake for
   25 minutes until the pastry is risen and
golden brown.

5 Remove from the oven and let stand for about
   10 minutes before turning out. Serve warm, cut
into wedges, with crème fraîche or sour cream.

Rhubarb, Orange
& Ginger Fool

Serves 4–6

1 pound young rhubarb
1 orange
3 tablespoons clear honey
2 tablespoons brown sugar
2 pieces stem ginger in syrup
1 cup fresh custard
½ cup heavy cream

1 Roughly chop the rhubarb and put in a saucepan. Grate the zest from the orange and add to the rhubarb. Peel off the skin and finely chop the flesh.

2 Add the honey and sugar to the rhubarb. Cover and cook for 10–15 minutes until the rhubarb is tender. Pour into a large bowl and let cool. Finely chop the stem ginger and stir in, along with the orange flesh.

3 Whip the custard and cream together and pour over the fruit. Chill until ready to serve.

Tip
You can also serve this dessert in individual glasses, decorated with toasted nuts and served with amaretti biscuits.

Berry Shortcake

Makes 8 shortcakes

5½ cups strawberries, hulled and
  sliced, or a mixture of strawberries,
  raspberries, blueberries, and
  blackberries
2–3 tablespoons granulated sugar
1–2 tablespoons raspberry juice or
  1 tablespoon orange juice
1 cup heavy cream, whipped until soft
  peaks formed and chilled

For the shortcake
1⅔ cups all-purpose flour, plus extra
  for dusting
2½ teaspoons baking powder
½ teaspoon salt
2 tablespoons granulated sugar,
  plus extra for sprinkling
¾ stick (6 tablespoons) butter, diced
1 cup heavy cream

To decorate
Sliced strawberries
Confectioners' sugar
Fresh mint leaves

1 Preheat the oven to 425°F. Put the berries in a large bowl and toss in the sugar and fruit juice. Let stand until the juices begin to run, stirring occasionally.

2 For the shortcake, mix the flour, baking powder, salt, and sugar together in a large bowl. Add the butter and rub it in until the mixture resembles coarse bread crumbs. Whip the cream and, using a fork, lightly stir in all but 1 tablespoon of it, little by little, until a soft dough is formed.

3 Turn out on to a lightly floured work surface and knead the dough 6–8 times. Pat or roll it into a rectangle about ½-inch thick. Using a round cutter, stamp out 8 rounds. Arrange 3 inches apart on a baking sheet. Brush the tops with the remaining cream and sprinkle with sugar.

4 Bake for 10 minutes until set and the tops are pale golden. Let cool on a wire rack.

5 Using a fork or serrated knife, split each shortcake horizontally. Put the bottoms on dessert plates and spoon the berry mixture equally over each. Spoon the chilled whipped cream over the berries. Top with the other half of shortcake and decorate each with a sliced strawberry, confectioners' sugar and a mint leaf.

Candied Fruit Bombe

Serves 6

¼ cup dark rum or brandy

1½ cups mixed dried fruit, such as apricots, raisins, figs, cherries, and cranberries, chopped

1 cup milk

1 vanilla bean

2 egg yolks

¼ cup granulated sugar

1 cup heavy cream

2 ounces good-quality semisweet chocolate, grated

Fresh mint sprigs, to decorate

Fresh figs, to serve

1 Pour the rum or brandy over the fruit and soak overnight. The next day, heat the milk and vanilla bean to simmering point in a saucepan over a low heat. Take off the heat and remove the vanilla bean. Whisk the egg yolks and sugar with a hand-held electric mixer until pale and slightly thickened, then whisk in the hot milk.

2 Return to a clean heavy-based, nonstick saucepan. Cook over a low heat, stirring continuously with a wooden spoon until the mixture thickens to the consistency of heavy cream and coats the back of a spoon. Cover with plastic wrap and let cool.

3 Lightly whip the cream until soft peaks form, then fold it into the cold custard. Freeze in a shallow freezerproof container for about 2–3 hours, or until half frozen, then whisk to break down any ice crystals and return to the freezer. Repeat this process at least twice more until the ice cream holds its shape. Alternatively, churn in an ice cream maker. Mix in the rum-soaked fruits and the chocolate.

4 Line a 1-quart deep mixing bowl or 6 individual bowls with plastic wrap. Spoon the mixture into the bowl and freeze until firm. Remove from the freezer 30 minutes before serving. Turn out and remove the plastic wrap. Decorate with mint sprigs and serve with fresh figs.

Fried Bananas with
Rum & Brown Sugar

Serves 2

⅓ stick (3 tablespoons) butter
2 bananas, peeled and
    halved lengthwise
2 tablespoons dark rum
2 tablespoons brown sugar
Whipped cream or ice cream,
    to serve

1 Melt the butter in a large skillet and add the bananas. Fry for 2 minutes on each side, until golden, then add the rum and let bubble.

2 Sprinkle the brown sugar over the top, then reduce the heat, stirring the sauce around the bananas until the sugar has dissolved completely.

3 Increase the heat, and allow the sauce to bubble again for a minute or so, until the sauce is syrupy. Serve with whipped cream or ice cream.

Cherry Syllabub

Serves 4

6 tablespoons sweet white wine
3 tablespoons white or coconut rum
2 tablespoons fresh lemon juice
½ cup granulated sugar
1 cup heavy cream
2 cups fresh cherries, pitted
Crisp almond biscuits, to serve

1 Combine the white wine, rum, lemon juice and sugar in a large bowl and mix well until the sugar has dissolved.

2 Stir in the cream and whip until soft peaks form. Spoon the cherries into the bases of 4 glasses and top with the cream syllabub.

3 Serve immediately with crisp almond biscuits to dip into the cream. If left to stand for too long the mixture will separate out again.

Tip
The joy of this dessert is that any flavored liqueur or spirit of your choice can be added to the basic mixture. Also the fruit can be varied depending on the season and your preference.

Prunes Steeped in Tea

with Vanilla

Serves 6

36 large prunes
2 cups water
2 heaping teaspoons dark tea leaves,
　such as Ceylon or Assam
½ cup granulated sugar
1 vanilla bean, split in half
　or 1 teaspoon pure vanilla extract
Vanilla ice cream, to serve (optional)

For the caramelized almonds
¾ cup flaked almonds
¼ cup granulated sugar

Tip
The steeped prunes can be stored in the refrigerator for several days.

1 Soak the prunes in hot water for at least 2 hours, then drain. Transfer to a large heatproof bowl.

2 Boil the water in a saucepan and add the tea. Turn off the heat and leave to steep for 10 minutes. Strain and pour the tea over the prunes, then stir in the sugar and vanilla bean or extract. Let the prunes steep for 2-3 hours, then chill until ready to serve.

3 For the caramelized almonds, combine the almonds and sugar in a non-stick saucepan. Put over a high heat, stirring continuously, for 2-3 minutes. When the almonds start to brown, pour them into a heatproof dish. When they are completely cool, break them up. Set aside.

4 Serve the prunes cold, with a little of the tea mixture. Add a scoop of vanilla ice cream, if liked, and top with the caramelized almonds.

Sweet & Nutty

Caramel Strawberries

Makes 24

1 cup, plus 2 tablespoons granulated sugar

3 tablespoons water

2 pints strawberries

3 tablespoons chopped, toasted hazelnuts

1 Put the sugar and water in a saucepan and heat gently until all the sugar has dissolved. Increase the heat and simmer for 6-10 minutes, or until golden. Take off the heat just before the caramel turns golden. If the caramel becomes too dark or smells burnt, plunge the base of the pan into a bowl of cold water to cool it down—being careful not to get any water into the caramel.

2 Take half the strawberries and, holding the strawberry by the stem, dip the lower half of each one in the caramel. Set on a baking sheet lined with parchment paper and let harden. If the caramel in the pan hardens, return it to a very low heat and swirl it around until it softens.

3 Take the remaining strawberries, and dip the lower half in the caramel as before, then roll in the chopped nuts. Let harden.

Pineapple Upside-down Cake

Serves 8

½ stick (4 tablespoons) butter
½ cup light brown sugar
14-ounce can pineapple rings in
    natural juice, drained, reserving
    5 tablespoons juice
7 red glacé cherries
2 tablespoons whole pecans (optional)
1 cup self-rising flour, sifted
1 teaspoon baking powder
Pinch of salt
1 cup, plus 2 tablespoons sugar
3 eggs, separated
½ teaspoon pure vanilla extract
¼ teaspoon pure almond extract
Evaporated milk or light cream,
    to serve

1 Preheat the oven to 350°F. Reserve 1 tablespoon of the butter, then melt the rest in a saucepan over a low heat. Pour into a 9-inch springform pan and sprinkle the brown sugar evenly over it. Arrange the pineapple rings in the butter-sugar mixture, putting a cherry in the center of each ring. Fill in the spaces with pecans. Sift the flour, baking powder, and salt together in another bowl. Cream the reserved 1 tablespoon of butter with the sugar in a separate bowl.

2 Beat the egg yolks in another bowl until pale, then slowly fold into the creamed mixture, continuing to beat until fluffy. Add the reserved pineapple juice, vanilla, and almond extracts and the flour mixture. Whisk the egg whites in a clean, grease-free bowl until stiff peaks form, then fold into the mixture.

3 Pour the mixture over the pineapple. Bake for 30–35 minutes. Let cool in the pan on a wire rack. Loosen the cake with a palette knife, cover with a serving plate and invert, so that the pineapple and cherry base with its runny, butterscotch topping is now on top. Remove the pan. Serve warm with evaporated milk or cream.

Summer Berry Galette

Serves 6

16 ounces puff pastry dough, thawed
    if frozen
Flour, for dusting

For the filling
1½ cups strawberries, hulled and
    sliced
1 cup raspberries
1¼ cups blueberries
3 tablespoons confectioners' sugar
⅓ cup ground almonds

1 Roll out the pastry on a lightly floured surface and cut a round 10 inches in diameter. Put on a baking sheet and chill for 20 minutes.

2 Preheat the oven to 400°F. For the filling, mix all the fruit together and stir in the confectioners' sugar. Sprinkle the ground almonds over the pastry and scatter the fruit on top, leaving a ½-inch margin around the edge.

3 Bake in the oven for 20 minutes until the pastry is golden. Let stand for 1–2 minutes before serving.

Tip
Lightly grease or oil the baking sheet before placing the pastry round on it, otherwise it may stick.

Muscat-poached Grapes
with Thick Creamy Yogurt

Serves 2

4 ounces black seedless grapes
1 cup Muscat dessert wine
2 tablespoons honey
1 vanilla bean, split lengthwise
1 cup Greek yogurt

1 Put the grapes, wine, honey, and vanilla bean in a saucepan and simmer for 5 minutes, or until the grapes have softened. Lift out the grapes using a slotted spoon and transfer them to a bowl.

2 Increase the heat and boil the syrup for 10 minutes, or until thick. Divide the yogurt between 2 serving glasses and top with the grapes and their syrup.

Tip
Use either grape juice, orange juice, or apple juice in place of the Muscat wine, if you prefer.

Spiced Baked Apples

Serves 4

6 large Golden Delicious apples
²/₃ stick (5 tablespoons) unsalted butter, softened
¼ cup packed light brown sugar
⅓ cup fresh white bread crumbs
1 green cardamom pod
½ teaspoon ground cinnamon
¼ teaspoon freshly grated nutmeg
Pinch of saffron strands
Finely grated zest of ½ lemon
3 tablespoons golden raisins
3 tablespoons shelled and chopped pistachio nuts
1¼ cups hard apple cider
Light cream, to serve

1 Preheat the oven to 400°F. Core the apples leaving them whole. Using a small sharp knife, make a horizontal cut around the middle of the apples—this will prevent the skin from bursting during cooking.

2 Cream the butter, sugar, and bread crumbs together in a medium bowl. Using a pestle and mortar, crush the cardamom pod and remove the black seeds. Alternatively, use the back of a spoon.

3 Add the seeds to the butter mixture together with the cinnamon, nutmeg, saffron, and lemon zest. Mix together well. Stir in the raisins and pistachio nuts.

4 Divide this mixture among the 6 apples, stuffing it down tightly into where the cores used to be and piling any excess mixture on top of the apples. Transfer the apples to a ceramic or glass ovenproof dish large enough to hold them all with a little space in between. Pour the cider around the apples.

5 Transfer the dish to the oven and bake for about 40-45 minutes, or until the apples are very tender.

6 Serve warm with the juices from the baking dish and some cold cream.

Strawberries in Pimm's

Syrup with Shortbread

Serves 2

½ cup Pimm's
½ cup orange juice
2 tablespoons granulated sugar
2 fresh mint sprigs
1½ cups strawberries, hulled and halved
4 shortbread cookies, to serve

1 Put the Pimm's, orange juice, sugar, and mint in a mixing bowl. Add the strawberries and leave them to macerate at room temperature for 30 minutes.

2 Serve the strawberries and juices in small bowls with the shortbread cookies.

Tip
Try using mixed summer berries instead of the strawberries and serve with amaretti biscuits.

Orange Terrine
with Citrus Cream

Serves 4–6

5 large oranges
2½ cups fresh orange juice
¼ cup granulated sugar
6 sheets leaf gelatin
Sunflower oil, for oiling

For the citrus cream
2 tablespoons confectioners' sugar
1¼ cups whipping cream
1 tablespoon orange flower water
Grated zest and juice of 1 lemon
Grated zest of 1 lime

1 Cut the oranges into segments and put in a bowl. Put the orange juice and sugar in a saucepan and heat to nearly boiling. Remove from the heat.

2 Add the gelatin to the heated orange juice and stir until dissolved. Let cool.

3 Lightly oil a 5-cup capacity terrine mold and put a layer of orange segments across the base.

Continue to layer until three-quarters full. Pour the orange juice in and let set in the refrigerator for at least 6 hours. Turn out on to a flat serving plate.

4 For the citrus cream, just before serving sift the confectioners' sugar into the cream, add the orange flower water and whip until soft peaks form. Stir in the lemon and lime zests, and the lemon juice. Serve with the terrine.

Tip
With a serrated knife, slice the stem end and bottom off the orange. Stand on one flat end and, following the curve of the orange, cut down the sides to remove the peel. Hold the orange in one hand and carefully cut down in between the membranes, releasing the segments which should now be clean and clear of any membranes.

Fresh Figs Baked

Serves 2

4 heaping tablespoons mascarpone
  cheese
1 tablespoon Amaretto liqueur
4 plump figs, halved
2 tablespoons granulated sugar
$\frac{1}{4}$ stick (2 tablespoons) unsalted butter,
  softened
2 tablespoons ground almonds
Pinch of freshly grated nutmeg

Tip

For an extra almond
flavor, sprinkle a few
toasted flaked almonds
over the top before
serving.

1 Mix the mascarpone and Amaretto liqueur together in a bowl until smooth. Set aside.

2 Preheat the broiler. Put the figs cut-side up on a baking sheet lined with parchment paper. Broil for 2 minutes, or until the flesh is softened.

3 Cream the sugar, butter, almonds, and nutmeg together in a bowl. Put a spoonful on each fig half and broil for 1–2 minutes, keeping a careful eye on them, because they will burn quite quickly.

4 Serve the hot figs at once with a spoonful of the flavored mascarpone.

Raspberry Surprise

Serves 4

3 egg whites
Pinch of salt
³/₄ cup granulated sugar
A drop of pure vanilla extract
1¹/₄ cups heavy cream
1 pint raspberries

1 Preheat the oven to 250°F. Line 2 baking sheets with parchment paper. Set aside.

2 Using an electric mixer, beat the egg whites and salt together in a clean, grease-free bowl until stiff. Check this by lifting the beaters from the mixture and holding it upside down. If the tip of the egg white falls, the peak is soft. If it stands firm, it is stiff.

3 Add about half the sugar and whisk thoroughly. Keep whisking until the egg whites no longer appear grainy and are shiny and smooth. Add more sugar, about 1 tablespoon at a time, beating well between additions until all of it has been added. Add the vanilla. Keep beating until smooth, thick, and glossy. If the sugar is not beaten in well enough, it will melt and leach out during cooking.

4 Put 8 large spoonfuls of the mixture on to the prepared baking sheets, leaving plenty of space in between. Transfer to the oven and bake for 1 hour, switching the baking sheets over halfway through, then switch off the oven and leave until cold. This will give the meringues a crisp outside and chewy, 'marshmallowy' inside. If you prefer them crisper, cook for 1¹/₂ hours, then leave until cold.

5 Roughly crush the meringues and set aside. Whip the cream in a large bowl until soft peaks form. Fold in the crushed meringues and raspberries. Serve immediately.

Tropical Fruit Salad

Serves 4

1-inch piece fresh ginger, peeled
1³/₄ cups water
2 cups, plus 2 tablespoons granulated
  sugar
1 star anise
1 lemon grass stalk
2 kaffir lime leaves
1 mango
1 papaya
2 firm pears
1 small cantaloupe melon

1 Finely chop the ginger and put in a large saucepan with the water and sugar. Add the star anise, lemon grass and lime leaves. Bring to a boil, then simmer quite fiercely for 20 minutes until the water has reduced and the liquid is quite syrupy. Remove the lemon grass and lime leaves and let cool.

2 Peel and cut the mango into wedges and put into a mixing bowl.

3 Halve the papaya lengthwise and scrape out the seeds. Peel carefully and cut into large wedges. Add to the mixing bowl.

4 Peel the pears and remove the core. Slice quite thickly and stir in with the other fruit.

5 Halve the melon and scrape out the seeds. Cut into quarters and remove the flesh from the rind. Cut into ¹/₂-inch slices. Put in the mixing bowl. Pour the syrup over the fruit and serve chilled.

Black Currant Pudding

Serves 4

½ stick (4 tablespoons) butter, at room temperature, plus extra for greasing

8 medium-thick slices of bread

1¾ cups fresh or frozen black currants or blackberries

5 eggs

⅓ cup granulated sugar

2½ cups whole milk or light cream

2 teaspoons pure vanilla extract

Pinch of freshly grated nutmeg, plus extra for sprinkling

1 tablespoon raw sugar, for sprinkling

Lightly whipped cream, to serve

1 Preheat the oven to 350°F. Grease a 5-cup baking dish.

2 Remove the crusts from the bread and discard. Spread the slices with the butter, then cut diagonally in half. Layer the bread slices in the dish, buttered-side up, scattering the black currants or blackberries between the layers as you go.

3 Whisk the eggs and sugar together lightly in a mixing bowl, then gradually whisk in the milk or cream, vanilla extract, and nutmeg.

4 Pour the mixture over the bread, pushing the slices down well to soak them thoroughly. Sprinkle over the raw sugar and some more nutmeg. Set the dish in a baking pan a quarter filled with hot water. Bake for 1 hour until the top is crisp and golden. Let cool slightly, then serve with lightly whipped cream.

Tarte Tatin

Serves 8

9 ounces puff pastry dough, thawed if
frozen
Flour, for dusting
Whipped cream or ice cream, to serve

For the filling
6 eating apples
1 tablespoon lemon juice
¾ stick (6½ tablespoons) butter
6 tablespoons granulated sugar

1 For the filling, peel, core, and slice the apples
into quarters, then use a fork to score the
rounded side. Cut each quarter in half widthwise,
then toss the pieces in the lemon juice.

2 Melt the butter in a 9-inch ovenproof skillet.
Stir in the sugar until it has melted, then
remove the pan from the heat.

3 Arrange the apple quarters, scored-side down,
in concentric circles in the pan. Pack them
quite tightly. Put the pan over a low heat and cook,
without disturbing the apples for 15 minutes, or
until they begin to caramelize.

4 Put a baking sheet in the oven and preheat to
400°F. Roll out the puff pastry dough on a
lightly floured surface to a round slightly larger
than the top of the skillet. Wrap it over the rolling
pin, then place it on top of the apples in the pan.
Tuck the edges inside the pan.

5 Transfer the skillet to the oven and bake the
tart for 20-25 minutes, or until the pastry is
well risen and golden brown.

6 Leave the tart to cool for 5 minutes, then ease a
knife between the top crust and the pan. Invert
a plate on top then carefully turn both pan and
plate over together so
that the apples are
on top. Serve
warm, with
whipped
cream or
ice cream.

Tip
Other types of fruit
can be used to make
similar tarts. Pears, plums,
nectarines, and apricots
work well, as does
rhubarb.

Berry Cornmeal Cake

Makes 8–10 slices

1¼ sticks (10 tablespoons) unsalted
   butter, softened, plus extra for
   greasing
¾ cup granulated sugar
¾ cup ground almonds
⅔ cup fine cornmeal
4 eggs, beaten
Finely grated zest and juice of 1 large
   lemon
1 teaspoon baking powder
⅔ cup raspberries
⅔ cup blueberries
Raw sugar, for sprinkling

1 Preheat the oven to 350°F. Grease and line an
8-inch round baking dish.

2 Beat the butter and sugar together in a bowl
until creamy. Add the ground almonds,
cornmeal, eggs, lemon zest and juice, and baking
powder and mix well. Add the raspberries and
blueberries and stir in gently to mix.

3 Spoon the mixture into the prepared dish and
level the surface. Bake in the oven for about
40 minutes, or until lightly browned and firm to
the touch.

4 Remove the cake from the oven and let cool
slightly. Sprinkle with raw sugar and serve
slightly warm or cold.

Seared Fruit in

Frothy Orange Sauce

Serves 4

2 fresh figs, cut into wedges

½ pineapple, peeled, cored, and cut
into chunks

1 ripe mango, peeled, pitted, and cut
into chunks

1⅓ cups blackberries

¼ cup white wine

5 tablespoons granulated sugar

6 egg yolks

2 tablespoons Cointreau or other
orange liqueur

Tip
Keep a close eye on
the fruit while they are
cooking under the
broiler as they are
liable to burn.

1 Divide the prepared fruit among 4 individual gratin dishes and scatter the blackberries over the top.

2 Heat the wine and sugar in a saucepan over a medium heat until the sugar has dissolved. Cook for 5 minutes.

3 Put the egg yolks in a large heatproof bowl. Set the bowl over a saucepan of simmering water and whisk the yolks until they have thickened and are pale and fluffy. Slowly pour the syrup into the egg yolks, with the Cointreau, whisking continuously until thickened.

4 Preheat the broiler. Spoon the frothy mixture over the fruit and broil until the topping is golden. Serve immediately.

Gooseberry Pie

Serves 6

1½ cups all-purpose flour, plus extra
    for dusting
Pinch of salt
½ cup fine cornmeal
¼ cup packed light brown sugar
1 stick, plus 1 tablespoon (9
    tablespoons) cold butter, diced
3–4 tablespoons cold water
1 egg, beaten
Whipped cream or custard, to serve

For the filling
5½ cups gooseberries
¼ cup granulated sugar, plus extra
    for dusting

1 Sift the flour and salt into a mixing bowl. Add the polenta and sugar, then add the butter and rub it in until the mixture resembles fine bread crumbs. Add 3 tablespoons cold water and mix to a firm dough, adding a little more water, if necessary. Knead briefly, then wrap in plastic wrap and chill for 20 minutes.

2 For the filling, mix the gooseberries with the sugar. Divide the dough into 2 pieces, one slightly larger than the other. Roll out the larger piece on a lightly floured surface and use to line an 8-inch shallow pie dish. Spoon the gooseberries into the dish. Brush the rim of the dough with a little beaten egg.

3 Roll out the remaining piece of dough and lay it over the gooseberries. Press down and seal the edges. Cut off any overhanging pastry, crimp the edges and snip a steam hole in the top of the pie. Chill for 20 minutes.

4 Preheat the oven to 375°F. Brush the top of the pie with a little more egg and dust with sugar. Bake for 40 minutes, or until golden brown. Serve warm with whipped cream or custard.

Pavlova with Tropical Fruits

Serves 4–6

3 egg whites
Pinch of salt
$^3/_4$ cup, plus 2 tablespoons granulated
  sugar
A drop of pure vanilla extract
1 teaspoon cornstarch
1 teaspoon distilled white vinegar
$^3/_4$ cup heavy cream

For the filling

1 large mango, peeled, pitted, and
  chopped
2 papayas, peeled and chopped
2 kiwi fruits, peeled and chopped
3 ripe passion fruit

1 Preheat the oven to 250°F. Line a baking sheet
with parchment paper. Set aside.

2 Using an electric mixer, beat the egg whites
and salt together in a clean bowl until stiff.
Check this by lifting the beaters from the
mixture and holding it upside down. If the tip
of the egg white falls, the peak is soft. If it stands
firm, it is stiff.

3 Add about half the sugar and whisk well. Keep
whisking until the egg white no longer appears
grainy and is shiny and smooth. Add more sugar,
about 1 tablespoon at a time, whisking thoroughly
between additions until all of it has been added.
Add the vanilla extract, cornstarch, and vinegar.
Keep whisking until the mixture is smooth, thick,
and glossy.

4 Spread the meringue mixture on to the
prepared baking sheet, in an 8-inch diameter
round, making a depression in the center. Transfer
to the oven and cook for 2 hours, then switch off
the oven and leave until cold.

5 Whip the cream until soft peaks form and use
to fill the meringue shell. Put the fruit on top,
then scoop the seeds from the passion fruit and
drizzle over the top. Serve immediately.

DINNER PARTY DELIGHTS

- Chocolate Profiteroles
- Tarte au Citron
- Butterscotch Torte
- Devil's Food Cake with Chocolate Orange Frosting
- Rhubarb & Custard Puff Pie
- Almond Pithiviers
- Champagne Jelly with Strawberries
- Passion Fruit Cheesecake
- Lemon Meringue Pie
- Burnt Custard
- Blueberry Streusel Tart
- Iced Summer Berries with Chocolate Sauce
- Chewy Meringues with Orange-scented Mascarpone
- Mango Sorbet
- Chocolate Truffles with Orange Flower Water

- Vanilla Poached Pears with Butterscotch Sauce
- Raspberry & Passion fruit Pavlova
- Summer Berry Tart
- Apple Pie
- Baked Peaches with Honey & Ricotta
- Crumble-topped Black currant Pie with Cinnamon Crust
- Spiced Palmiers with Apples & Raisins
- Persimmon & Passion Fruit Ice Cream
- Apple & Calvados Soufflé
- Baked Lemon Custards with Brandy Snaps
- Crème Brûlée with Lemon & Lime Shorties
- Crêpes Suzette
- Hazelnut Meringue Cake

CHAPTER SIX

DINNER PARTY DELIGHTS

Chocolate Profiteroles

Makes 12

1 cup all-purpose flour
1 tablespoon confectioners' sugar
About $^3/_4$ cup water
$^2/_3$ stick (5 tablespoons) butter, diced
3 eggs, beaten
$1^1/_4$ cups heavy cream
2 tablespoons hot cocoa mix

For the sauce
$4^1/_2$ ounces good-quality semisweet
   chocolate, broken into pieces
2 tablespoons light corn syrup
2 tablespoons butter
$^1/_4$ cup water

1 Preheat the oven to 400°F. Sift the flour and confectioners' sugar into a small bowl. Put the water and butter in a saucepan and heat gently until the butter has melted. Bring to a boil, then remove from the heat and quickly add the flour mixture, beating until smooth. Transfer to a bowl and let cool.

2 With a hand-held electric mixer, gradually beat the eggs into the mixture to make choux pastry. Fit a piping bag with a plain nozzle and fill with the paste. Pipe 12 rounds onto a nonstick baking sheet. Bake for 18–20 minutes until puffed and golden. Make a hole in the base of each profiterole and let cool on a wire rack.

3 Whip the cream with the chocolate powder until stiff. Fill a new piping bag with the chocolate cream and pipe carefully into the hole in the base of each individual profiterole.

4 For the sauce, put the chocolate, corn syrup, butter, and water into a bowl and set over a saucepan of simmering water. Melt the chocolate and stir to mix. To serve, drizzle the warm chocolate sauce over the profiteroles.

Tarte au Citron

Serves 8

1 cup, plus 2 tablespoons all-purpose
  flour, plus extra for dusting
Pinch of salt
⅔ stick (5 tablespoons) cold butter
1 tablespoon granulated sugar
1 egg yolk
1 tablespoon cold water
Confectioners' sugar, for dusting

For the filling
3 large lemons
5 eggs, lightly beaten
¼ stick (2 tablespoons) unsalted butter,
  melted
¾ cup granulated sugar

1 Sift the flour and salt into a mixing bowl. Add the butter and rub it in until the mixture resembles bread crumbs. Stir in the sugar. Mix the egg yolk and water together, then sprinkle over the dry mixture and mix to a firm dough. Knead briefly, then wrap in plastic wrap and chill for 1 hour.

2 Preheat the oven to 400°F. Roll the pastry out on a floured surface and use to line an 8½-inch round or 13 x 5-inch rectangular loose-bottomed tart pan. Prick the base all over.

3 Line the tart shell with parchment paper and fill with baking beans. Bake for 15 minutes. Remove the paper and beans, brush the inside of the case with 2 teaspoons of the beaten egg from the filling. Bake for 5 minutes. Reduce the temperature to 250°F.

4 Grate the zest from the lemons. Squeeze the juice; you will need ⅔ cup. Put the lemon zest and juice in a bowl with the eggs, butter, and sugar. Beat until smooth.

5 Pour the filling into the tart shell and bake for 35–45 minutes, or until just set. Transfer the pan to a wire rack and leave for 10 minutes before removing the tart from the pan. Let cool, then chill. Dust with confectioners' sugar before serving.

Butterscotch Torte

Serves 8

2 sticks (16 tablespoons) butter, at
room temperature

1 cup, plus 2 tablespoons granulated
sugar

4 eggs, beaten

2 teaspoons pure vanilla extract

1⅓ cups self-rising flour, sifted

For the filling

1 stick (8 tablespoons) butter

1 cup packed dark brown sugar

⅓ cup boiling water

1½ cups heavy cream

1 cup milk

3 tablespoons cornstarch

1 Preheat the oven to 375°F. Butter and line three
8-inch cake pans with parchment paper.

2 Beat the butter with the sugar until light and
fluffy. Beat in the eggs, little by little, and fold in
the vanilla and flour. Spoon into the cake pans and
level off the top. Bake 20–25 minutes until firm,
springy, and golden. Turn out on to wire racks and
let cool.

3 For the filling, melt the butter in a saucepan and
stir in the sugar. Boil for 1 minute, then stir in the
water—be careful, it will bubble up. Remove from
the heat. Heat ½ cup of the cream with the milk in a
separate saucepan until it reaches boiling point.

4 In a large bowl, mix the cornstarch with a little
water. Add the hot cream and milk mixture and
stir well. Whisk into the melted butter and sugar
and cook for 1 minute over a low heat until thick.
Set aside to cool completely.

5 Whip the remaining cream to soft peaks. Place
one cake layer on a serving plate. Spread over a
third of the butterscotch filling and cover with a
third of the whipped cream. Press a second cake
layer on top and repeat with the fillings.

6 Top with the final cake layer and cover with
the remaining butterscotch and cream. This
cake will not keep for long and is best served on
the day of baking.

Devil's Food Cake

with Chocolate Orange Frosting

Makes 8–10 slices

1¼ sticks (10 tablespoons) unsalted
   butter, softened, plus extra for
   greasing
6 ounces semisweet chocolate, broken
   into squares
½ cup granulated sugar
6 large eggs, separated
⅔ cup all-purpose flour
⅓ cup ground almonds

For the frosting
1 cup whipping cream
6½ ounces semisweet chocolate,
   broken into squares
2 teaspoons finely grated orange zest
Candied orange slices, to decorate

1 Preheat the oven to 350°F. Grease and line a
   deep 8-inch round cake pan.

2 For the cake, melt the chocolate in a heatproof
   bowl set over a saucepan of simmering water.
Remove and cool slightly. Beat the butter and half of
the sugar together in a separate bowl until creamy.
Beat in the melted chocolate, then beat in the egg
yolks, one at a time.

3 Sift the flour and ground almonds into a
   separate bowl. Beat the egg whites in a clean
bowl until stiff, then gradually beat in the remaining
sugar. Stir half of the beaten egg whites into the
chocolate mixture to loosen it slightly, then fold in
the flour mixture together with the remaining
beaten egg whites.

4 Spoon the mixture into the prepared pan
   and level the surface. Bake in the oven for
50–60 minutes, or until a skewer inserted into
the center comes out clean. Cool in the pan for
10 minutes, then turn out on to a wire rack and
let cool completely.

5 For the frosting, heat the cream in a saucepan
   until nearly boiling. Remove from the heat,
stir in the chocolate until melted, then stir in
the orange zest. Keep stirring until thick. Spread
the frosting over the top and sides of the cake.
Decorate with candied orange slices, then let the
frosting set before serving.

Rhubarb & Custard Puff Pie

Serves 4–6

12 ounces puff pastry dough, thawed if
   frozen
Flour, for dusting
1 egg, beaten
2 tablespoons confectioners' sugar,
   for dusting

For the filling

12 ounces young rhubarb, cut into
   2-inch pieces
$\frac{1}{3}$ cup sugar
$1\frac{1}{3}$ cups prepared custard (p.131)
1 teaspoon pure vanilla extract

1 Preheat the oven to 350°F. For the filling, put the
rhubarb in an ovenproof dish and sprinkle over
the sugar. Cover and bake for 40 minutes, or until
tender. Let cool.

2 Mix the custard and vanilla extract together in
a bowl, then carefully stir in the rhubarb, being
careful not to break the fruit.

3 Roll out the puff pastry dough on a lightly
floured surface to form a 12 x 15-inch
rectangle and put on a nonstick baking sheet.
Pile the custard and rhubarb mixture on to one
half leaving a 1-inch margin and brush with a little
beaten egg.

4 Fold the dough half over the filling and press
down to seal the edges—crimp with your
fingers or the back of a fork. Brush the top with a
little more egg. Sift the sugar evenly over the top.

5 Bake the pie in the oven for 25–30 minutes
until risen and golden. Let stand for 5 minutes
before serving.

Almond Pithiviers

Serves 8

12 ounces puff pastry dough, thawed if
   frozen
Flour, for dusting
1 egg, beaten
1 tablespoon confectioners' sugar,
   for dusting

For the filling

1 cup milk
1 teaspoon pure vanilla extract
3 egg yolks
$3/4$ cup granulated sugar
1 heaping tablespoon cornstarch
1 stick (8 tablespoons) unsalted butter,
   softened
1 cup ground almonds

1 For the filling, put the milk and vanilla extract in a saucepan and slowly bring to a boil. Mix the egg yolks, $1/4$ cup of the sugar, and cornstarch together in a bowl. Pour the vanilla-flavored milk over the egg yolk mixture and stir.

2 Return the mixture to the pan and cook over a low heat, stirring for 1 minute, or until thick. Remove from the heat and let cool.

3 Beat the butter and $1/2$ cup of the sugar together until light and fluffy. Stir in the ground almonds, then fold in the cold custard.

4 Divide the puff pastry dough into 2 pieces. Roll out one piece on a lightly floured surface to $1/4$-inch thick and cut out a 10-inch round. Put on a nonstick baking sheet and spread the almond mixture over the pastry, leaving a 1-inch margin around the edge. Brush the edge with beaten egg.

5 Roll out the remaining dough to the same thickness and cut an $11^{1}/_{2}$-inch round. Lay it over the almond-topped pastry and press down to seal the edges. Chill for 30 minutes.

6 Preheat the oven to 400°F. Brush the surface with beaten egg and score the top in a diamond pattern with the tip of a very sharp knife. Bake for 35–40 minutes until golden. Let stand for 5 minutes before dusting with confectioners' sugar and serving.

Tip
This dessert is best eaten on the day it is made. Serve with some vanilla ice cream, if liked.

Champagne Jelly
with Strawberries

Serves 2

½ cup, plus 2 tablespoons granulated
  sugar
⅔ cup water
⅔ cup champagne
3 sheets gelatin, soaked in ¼ cup water
Strawberries and light cream, to serve

1 Put the sugar and water in a small saucepan over a low heat and stir until dissolved. Increase the heat and boil for about 5 minutes, or until syrupy.

2 Take the pan off the heat and add just enough of the champagne to cool the syrup slightly. Beat in the soaked gelatin, until it has completely dissolved, then pour in the remaining champagne.

3 Pour the mixture into two ⅔-cup molds or one 1⅓-cup mold, and put in the refrigerator to set. Unmold by inverting on to a plate and giving the mold a short, sharp shake. Serve with fresh strawberries and cream.

Tip
Before adding the champagne and gelatin in step 2, make sure the syrup is hot enough to melt the gelatin but cool enough not to cook it, otherwise the jelly will not set properly.

Passion Fruit Cheesecake

Serves 8–10

1¼ cups graham cracker crumbs
¾ stick (6 tablespoons) butter, melted
9 ripe passion fruits, halved
1½ pounds cream cheese
1 cup, plus 2 tablespoons sugar
½ cup light cream
4 eggs, beaten
3 egg yolks
2 teaspoons pure vanilla extract

1 Combine the graham cracker crumbs and the melted butter. Press the mixture into the base of a 9-inch springform cake pan and chill for 20 minutes until firm. Cover the outside of the pan with a layer of aluminum foil.

2 Preheat the oven to 325°F. Put a sieve over a bowl and spoon in the pulp from 6 of the passion fruits. With the back of a wooden spoon extract as much juice from the seeds as possible.

3 Put the cream cheese, sugar, and cream in a food processor and process until smooth. Pour in the eggs and egg yolks and process again until well mixed. Add the vanilla extract and passion fruit juice and process briefly. Pour the cheesecake mixture into the pan.

4 Put the pan in a shallow dish and pour in enough water to come quarter-way up the sides of the pan. Bake for 1½ hours until just firm. (The aluminum foil around the pan will stop the water from leaking into the cheesecake.) Turn off the oven and leave the cheesecake in the oven for an extra 10 minutes.

5 Chill the cheesecake for at least 3–4 hours. Once firm, remove the sides of the pan. Spoon the pulp from the remaining passion fruits over the cheesecake just before serving.

Lemon Meringue Pie

Serves 8

9-inch baked pie crust

For the filling
1 cup, plus 2 tablespoons granulated
    sugar
2½ tablespoons cornstarch
1 cup boiling water
3 egg yolks, lightly beaten
¼ stick (2 tablespoons) butter
Finely grated zest and juice of
    2 large lemons

For the meringue
3 egg whites, at room temperature
¼ teaspoon cream of tartar
6 tablespoons granulated sugar
½ teaspoon pure vanilla extract

1 Preheat the oven to 450°F. For the filling, combine the sugar and cornstarch over a low heat and slowly add the boiling water, stirring continuously. Bring to a boil, then simmer still stirring for about 5 minutes until the mixture becomes transparent and thickens.

2 Put the lightly beaten egg yolks in a separate bowl. Remove the sugar and cornstarch mixture from the heat and gradually pour the hot liquid into the yolks. Set the bowl over a saucepan of simmering water. Stir in the butter, lemon juice, and zest and continue to cook until the filling becomes very thick. Let cool, then pour into the pie crust.

3 For the meringue, beat the egg whites in a clean bowl until frothy. Add the cream of tartar and continue beating. Drizzle in the sugar and vanilla extract and continue beating until stiff peaks form. Take care not to overbeat.

4 Pile the meringue on to the lemon filling, swirling lightly from the center towards the edges, ensuring that it touches the pastry all around. Use the tip of a knife to gently pull the meringue into peaks. Bake in the center of the oven for about 10–15 minutes until the meringue is a delicate brown. Serve warm.

Burnt Custard

Serves 4

1³/₄ cup heavy cream
1 vanilla bean, split in half
5 egg yolks
¹/₂ cup granulated sugar
¹/₄ cup bourbon

Tip

If using a blow torch to caramelize the top, make sure you use a culinary blow torch available from kitchenware shops.

1 Preheat the oven to 400°F. Heat the cream and vanilla bean in a saucepan over a low heat until almost boiling, then leave to infuse for 10 minutes. Whisk the egg yolks with 5 tablespoons sugar in a bowl until pale and thickened slightly. Stir in the hot vanilla cream and bourbon.

2 Pour into four 5-ounce ramekins and put them in a roasting pan. Pour in warm water to come halfway up the sides. Bake for 12–15 minutes until a skin has formed, but the custard is still wobbly.

3 Chill the ramekins at least 3 hours. Preheat the broiler. Scatter the remaining sugar over the tops. Cook under the hot broiler or use a blow torch to caramelise the sugar. Let the caramel cool before serving.

Blueberry Streusel Tart

Serves 8

1 stick (8 tablespoons) butter, softened,
 plus extra for greasing
3 tablespoons granulated sugar
1 egg
2¼ cups all-purpose flour
¼ cup light cream
½ teaspoon pure vanilla extract
2 tablespoons finely ground almonds
2 tablespoons soft white bread crumbs
Plain yogurt, to serve

For the filling
2½ pints blueberries
½ cup granulated sugar
5 tablespoons soft white bread crumbs
3 tablespoons flaked almonds
2 tablespoons light brown sugar
½ teaspoon ground cinnamon

1 Put a baking sheet in the oven and preheat to 400°F. Grease a 10½-inch tart pan. Beat the butter and sugar together in a bowl. When the mixture is light and fluffy, beat in the egg with a little of the flour.

2 Stir in the remaining flour alternately with the cream and vanilla extract, mixing to a smooth, soft dough. Spoon the dough into the pan, then gently ease it evenly across the base of the pan and up the sides.

3 Mix the ground almonds and bread crumbs together, and sprinkle the mixture evenly in the tart shell.

4 For the filling, mix the blueberries with the sugar and half the bread crumbs. Spoon the mixture into the tart shell.

5 Mix the remaining bread crumbs, flaked almonds, brown sugar, and cinnamon together in another bowl. Scatter the mixture evenly over the blueberries.

6 Bake for 30 minutes, or until the pastry is cooked and the streusel topping is golden. Serve warm with yogurt.

Iced Summer Berries
with Chocolate Sauce

Serves 4

3 cups mixed summer berries, such
as strawberries, blueberries,
raspberries, or blackberries
1 cup heavy cream
1 teaspoon pure vanilla extract
2½ ounces white chocolate,
broken into pieces

1 Put the berries in a large flat dish and freeze for
45 minutes.

2 Heat the cream and vanilla extract in a
saucepan until it reaches boiling point. Add the
chocolate and stir until melted and the sauce is
smooth. Pour into a small pitcher and serve warm
with the iced berries.

Tip

For a dark sauce,
replace the white
chocolate with the same
quantity of milk
chocolate.

Chewy Meringues

with Orange-scented Mascarpone

Makes 2

3 egg whites
³/₄ cup sugar
½ teaspoon distilled white vinegar
1 heaping teaspoon cornstarch

For the topping
½ cup mascarpone cheese
3 tablespoons orange juice
Zest of 1 orange
½ pomegranate

1 Preheat the oven to 275°F. Put the egg whites in a clean, grease-free bowl and beat until stiff. Add 5 tablespoons of the sugar, a tablespoon at a time, beating after each addition until glossy. Add the remaining sugar and beat gently. Mix the vinegar and cornstarch together in a small bowl and stir into the mixture.

2 Spoon the mixture onto parchment paper to make two 4-inch rounds. Bake for 1 hour, then let cool.

3 Meanwhile, mix the mascarpone, orange juice and zest together. Bash the back of the pomegranate with a rolling pin to remove the seeds. Top the meringues with the mascarpone mixture and scatter the pomegranate seeds on top. Serve immediately.

Mango Sorbet

Serves 8

2 cups water
2¼ cups granulated sugar
1 vanilla bean, split lengthwise
15 ounces fresh, canned, or frozen
   mango pieces
Juice of 1 lime
2 tablespoons stem ginger, chopped
Fresh mint sprigs, to decorate
Dessert cookies, to serve

1 Pour the water into a saucepan and add the sugar and vanilla bean. Bring to a boil and simmer for 2 minutes.

2 Remove the pan from the heat and let cool completely. When ready to use, remove the vanilla bean, split it in half and scrape down the inside to remove the seeds. Put the seeds into the syrup and discard the empty bean.

3 Put the mango in a blender and purée, or mash well by hand. Add the lime juice and vanilla syrup and mix well.

4 If using an ice cream maker, follow the manufacturer's instructions to make a sorbet. If making by hand, pour the mixture into a freezerproof container and freeze for 4 hours. Beat in a food processor until smooth, then return to the container and freeze again.

5 When firm, scoop the sorbet into bowls and top with stem ginger. Decorate with a mint sprig, and serve with cookies.

White Chocolate Truffles
with Orange Flower Water

Makes 10

1/3 cup heavy cream
5 ounces white chocolate
1–2 tablespoons orange flower water
1/4 cup cocoa powder

Tip

For dark chocolate truffles, replace the white chocolate with semisweet or bittersweet and use brandy instead of the orange flower water.

1 Heat the cream in a small saucepan until almost boiling. Take off the heat, let cool for 5 minutes, or until warm enough to touch, then stir in the chocolate and orange flower water until smooth.

2 Dust your hands in a little cocoa and put the remainder on a flat plate. Scoop out a walnut-sized piece of chocolate with a spoon and roll it in your hands. Roll in cocoa and put on a clean plate. Repeat with the remaining mixture. Chill for 1 hour to firm up before serving.

Vanilla Poached Pears

with Butterscotch Sauce

Serves 6

6 ripe pears, peeled
3–4 cups water
1 cup granulated sugar
2 vanilla beans, split lengthwise
Pared zest of 1/2 lemon
Vanilla ice cream or whipped cream, to
serve (optional)

For the sauce
1/2 stick (4 tablespoons) butter
1/3 cup packed light brown sugar
1/2 cup light corn syrup
1/2 cup heavy cream

1 Stand the pears in a saucepan just big enough for them to fit snugly. Pour enough water over to just cover and add the sugar, vanilla beans, and lemon zest.

2 Bring to a boil, then reduce the heat and simmer for 40-50 minutes until the pears are softened but still hold their shape. (If the pears aren't very ripe this might take a bit longer.) Remove from the heat and let the pears cool in the syrup.

3 For the butterscotch sauce, melt the butter with the brown sugar and corn syrup. Stir in 1/2 cup of the cooled pear syrup and simmer for 2-3 minutes. Stir in the cream and simmer for a further 2-3 minutes.

4 Remove the pears to a serving dish and either pour a little butterscotch sauce over each pear, or serve it separately in a small pitcher. Serve with vanilla ice cream or whipped cream.

Raspberry & Passion Fruit

Pavlova

Serves 4–6

4 egg whites
1 cup, plus 2 tablespoons granulated
  sugar
1 teaspoon distilled white vinegar
1½ teaspoons cornstarch
1 teaspoon pure vanilla extract

For the topping
2½ cups heavy cream
3 cups fresh raspberries
4 ripe passion fruit
Fresh mint sprigs
Confectioners' sugar for dusting

1 Preheat the oven to 350°F. Line a baking sheet with parchment paper. Beat the egg whites in a clean bowl until stiff. Beat in the sugar 1 tablespoon at a time, whisking between each addition.

2 Blend the vinegar, cornstarch, and vanilla extract together in a small bowl, then whisk into the meringue mixture.

3 Spoon the mixture onto the paper-lined baking sheet and spread out to a 10-inch round. Make a slight dip in the center. Bake for 5 minutes. Reduce the oven temperature to 300°F, then bake for 1¼ hours, or until firm to the touch and lightly golden. Turn off the oven and let cool in the oven for 2–3 hours.

4 Slide a palette knife under the pavlova and transfer to a flat serving plate. Whip the cream until soft peaks form and spoon into the center of the pavlova.

5 Scatter the raspberries over the top. Scoop the seeds and pulp out of the passion fruit and scatter on to the raspberries. Decorate with mint sprigs and dust with confectioners' sugar.

Summer Berry Tart

Serves 6–8

2 cups, plus 2 tablespoons all-purpose
 flour, plus extra for dusting
3 tablespoons confectioners' sugar
1½ sticks (12 tablespoons) cold butter
2 egg yolks
¼ cup cold water
Confectioners' sugar, for dusting

For the filling
2½ cups milk
4 egg yolks
⅓ cup sugar
3 tablespoons flour
3 tablespoons cornstarch
Grated zest of 1 orange
⅔ cup heavy cream
3½ cups mixed summer berries, such
 as raspberries, strawberries,
 blueberries, and red currants

1 Sift the flour and confectioners' sugar into a
 mixing bowl. Add the butter and rub it in until
the mixture resembles bread crumbs. Whisk the egg
yolks with the cold water. Make a well in the center
of the flour, add the egg mixture and mix to a firm
dough. Knead briefly, then wrap in plastic wrap and
chill for 20 minutes.

2 Roll out the dough on a lightly floured surface
 and use to line a 10-inch loose-bottomed tart
pan. Prick the base and chill for 10 minutes.

3 Preheat the oven to 375°F. Line the tart shell
 with parchment paper and fill with baking
beans. Bake for 20 minutes until golden and crisp.
Remove the paper and beans and let cool on a
wire rack.

4 For the filling, pour the milk into a nonstick
 saucepan and bring to a boil. Mix the egg yolks
with the sugar, and stir in the flour and cornstarch.
Pour the mixture into the hot milk and mix well.

5 Bring the milk mixture to a boil, stirring
 continuously to prevent lumps forming. Once
the custard is thick and smooth, remove from the
heat and stir in the orange zest. Cover and chill.

6 Whip the cream in a bowl until soft peaks
 form, then fold into the cold custard. Spoon the
custard into the tart shell and level off. Arrange the
mixed summer fruit over the custard and dust with
confectioners' sugar before serving.

Apple Pie

Serves 8

3¹⁄₃ cups all-purpose flour, plus extra
    for dusting
½ teaspoon salt
1 stick (8 tablespoons) butter
6½ tablespoons shortening
Cold water
Milk, for glazing
Granulated sugar, for dusting

For the filling

1 pound pie apples, such as Granny
    Smith, peeled, cored, and thinly sliced
2 teaspoons lemon juice
6 tablespoons raisins
1 teaspoon pared orange zest
1 cup packed light brown sugar
4 teaspoons cornstarch
1 teaspoon ground cinnamon
1 teaspoon freshly grated nutmeg
4 teaspoons butter

1 Sift the flour and salt into a mixing bowl. Add the butter and shortening and rub them in until the mixture resembles bread crumbs. Add just enough cold water and mix to a firm dough. Knead briefly, then wrap in plastic wrap and let chill for 30 minutes.

2 Put a baking sheet in the oven and preheat to 400°F. For the filling, put the sliced apples into a bowl. Toss with the lemon juice, then add all the remaining filling ingredients, except the butter, and mix lightly.

3 Roll out just less than half the dough on a lightly floured surface and use to line a 10-inch pie dish. Add the filling, mounding it into the center, then dot with the butter.

4 Roll out the remaining dough and make a lid for the pie. Seal and crimp the edges and snip 2 steam vents. Brush the surface lightly with milk and sprinkle with sugar. Bake for 15 minutes, then reduce the oven temperature to 350°F and bake for a further 20 minutes. Serve hot or cold.

Baked Peaches
with Honey & Ricotta

Serves 2

2 ripe peaches
4 tablespoons ricotta cheese
2 tablespoons Amaretto liqueur
2 tablespoons honey
Red currant sprigs, to decorate
  (optional)

1 Preheat the oven to 400°F. Halve the peaches and carefully pry out the pits using the point of a knife. Put the peaches cut-side up in a small roasting pan and put a tablespoon of ricotta cheese in the center of each half.

2 Mix the Amaretto and honey together in a small bowl, then drizzle the mixture over the peaches and ricotta.

3 Bake for 10-15 minutes, then spoon into bowls and drizzle over any juices from the roasting pan. Serve hot, topped with sprigs of red currants.

Tip
Advance preparation:
The topping will keep in a covered container in the refrigerator for up to 2 days. Bake the fruit, cover, and refrigerate the day of serving. Assemble the dessert just before serving.

Crumble-topped

Black currant Pie with Cinnamon Pastry

Serves 6–8

1¾ cups all-purpose flour, plus extra
  for dusting
Pinch of salt
1 teaspoon ground cinnamon
1 stick (8 tablespoons) butter, diced
3–4 tablespoons cold water
Whipped cream, to serve

For the filling
5½ cups black currants
⅓ cup sugar

For the crumble topping
1⅓ cups all-purpose flour
Pinch of salt
1 stick (8 tablespoons) butter, diced
⅓ cup packed light brown sugar
½ cup flaked almonds

1 Sift the flour, salt and cinnamon into a mixing bowl. Add the butter and rub it in until the mixture resembles bread crumbs. Add just enough water and mix to a firm dough. Knead briefly, then wrap and chill for 30 minutes.

2 Roll out the dough on a lightly floured surface to line a 9-inch loose-bottomed tart pan. Prick the pastry and chill for 10 minutes.

3 Preheat the oven to 400°F. Line the pie shell with parchment paper and fill with baking beans. Bake for about 20 minutes. Remove the paper and beans and bake for 10 minutes until pale golden. Let cool.

4 Mix the black currants and sugar together in a bowl and set aside.

5 For the crumble topping, put the flour and salt into a large bowl. Add the butter and rub it in until coarsely combined, with largish lumps of butter still showing. Stir in the brown sugar.

6 Spoon the black currants into the pie shell and top evenly with the crumb mixture. Sprinkle over the flaked almonds. Bake for 20–25 minutes until golden and bubbling. Serve warm with whipped cream.

Spiced Palmiers

with Apples & Raisins

Makes about 36 biscuits

For the palmiers
15 ounces puff pastry dough, thawed if
    frozen
Flour, for dusting
$1/4$ cup granulated sugar
2 tablespoons confectioners' sugar
1 teaspoon ground cinnamon
$1/2$ teaspoon ground ginger
$1/2$ teaspoon freshly grated nutmeg
$2/3$ cup whipped cream, to serve

For the apple and raisin compote
1 pound apples, roughly chopped
$1/4$ cup granulated sugar
1 tablespoon raisins
1 tablespoon cranberries
2 teaspoons grated orange zest

1 Roll the puff pastry dough out thinly on a lightly floured surface and trim to a 10 x 16-inch rectangle. Cut the pastry in two to make two smaller rectangles. Sift the granulated sugar, confectioners' sugar, and spices together. Dust both sides of both pastry sheets with about a quarter of the spiced sugar.

2 Working one rectangle at a time, lay the pastry in front of you with one long edge nearest you. Fold the pastry in half, away from you, then unfold to give a crease down the middle. Fold the edge of the pastry nearest you halfway to the crease and repeat with the edge of the pastry furthest from you. Dust liberally with the spiced sugar.

3 Repeat the fold so the edge nearest you meets the edge furthest from you in the middle where you creased the pastry originally. Dust with sugar and reserve any leftover. Fold again down the crease to give a long thin rectangle. This will give you 6 layers. Repeat with the second rectangle. Wrap each in plastic wrap and freeze for 1 hour.

4 Preheat the oven to 350°F. Dust the pastry with any remaining sugar. Cut each crosswise into 18 slices. Lay the slices on a baking sheet and bake for 10 minutes, then turn and bake for 5–10 minutes until golden. Cool.

5 Put all the compote ingredients in a saucepan. Cover and cook over a low heat for 15 minutes. Stir and cool. Serve the palmiers with the compote and whipped cream.

Persimmon & Passion Fruit

Ice Cream

Serves 4

3 ripe persimmons
3 ripe passion fruits, halved
Juice of 1 lemon
5 tablespoons granulated sugar
1¼ cups heavy cream
Extra passion fruit pulp, to serve

1 Cut the top off each persimmon and spoon the persimmon flesh into a bowl, using a teaspoon to scrape as much flesh off the skins as possible. Put a strainer over the bowl. Scrape the passion fruit pulp into the sieve, then press it through with the back of a spoon, leaving the black seeds behind.

2 Spoon the mixture into a food processor, add the lemon juice and sugar and process to a fine purée. With the motor running, gradually add the cream until well combined.

3 Pour into a freezerproof container and freeze for about 2–3 hours, or until half-frozen, then beat to break up any ice crystals. Repeat this process twice more until the ice cream holds its shape. Alternatively, churn in an ice cream maker.

4 Before serving, let the ice cream soften for 20–30 minutes. Serve in scoops with a little passion fruit pulp spooned over the top.

Apple & Calvados Soufflé

Serves 6

3 tablespoons butter, plus extra
    for greasing
1 tablespoon graham cracker crumbs
$\frac{1}{3}$ cup all-purpose flour
$\frac{3}{4}$ cup milk
3 tablespoons Calvados or other
    apple brandy
2 tart apples, peeled, cored, and sliced
2 teaspoons grated lemon zest
2 tablespoons fresh lemon juice
$\frac{1}{2}$ cup, plus 2 tablespoons granulated
    sugar
4 eggs, separated
Confectioners' sugar, for dusting

1 Preheat the oven to 375°F. Grease six 1$\frac{1}{4}$-cup soufflé dishes or a 2-quart soufflé dish and scatter the cracker crumbs around the sides and over the base.

2 Melt the remaining butter in a saucepan and add the flour. Remove from the heat and gradually stir in the milk. Return the pan to the heat and bring to a boil, whisking gently until the mixture thickens. Cook for 1 minute, then remove from the heat and whisk in the Calvados. Cover the sauce and set aside to cool.

3 Cook the apples with the lemon zest and juice and 1 tablespoon of the granulated sugar in a covered saucepan, stirring occasionally, for 5–6 minutes until softened. Transfer to a blender or food processor and process until puréed, then let cool slightly. Meanwhile, whisk the egg yolks into the cooled sauce, then stir in the apple purée.

4 Beat the egg whites in a clean, grease-free bowl until stiff. Gradually beat in the remaining sugar until the mixture is glossy. Stir a spoonful of the whites into the sauce, then fold in the rest. Spoon the mixture into the individual soufflé dishes or large soufflé dish. Wipe the top of the dishes and bake for 20–35 minutes, depending on the size of the dish. Resist the temptation to open the oven door while cooking. Dust the top with confectioners' sugar before serving.

Baked Lemon Custards
with Brandy Snaps

Serves 6

2½ cups heavy cream
8 egg yolks
1⅓ cups confectioners' sugar, sifted
Juice of 4 lemons

For the brandy snaps
1 stick (8 tablespoons) butter, plus
   extra for greasing
½ cup, plus 2 tablespoons granulated
   sugar
¼ cup light corn syrup
1 cup all-purpose flour
Juice of 1 lemon
Pinch of ground ginger

1 Preheat the oven to 300°F. Mix the cream, egg yolks, confectioners' sugar, and lemon juice together in a bowl and pour into 6 ramekins. Half-fill a roasting pan with hot water and put the ramekins in the pan. Bake for 1 hour. Remove and let chill for 4 hours.

2 Preheat the oven to 375°F. For the brandy snaps, grease a large baking sheet and the handles of 6 wooden spoons or something of a similar size.

3 Melt the butter, sugar, and corn syrup in a saucepan. Remove from the heat and stir in the flour, lemon juice, and ground ginger.

4 Put teaspoons of the mixture on the baking sheet, making sure you leave a gap of at least 6 inches as the mixture spreads during cooking. Bake for 5–6 minutes until golden brown. Set aside the brandy snaps for a few minutes until cool enough to handle. Shape each one around the handle of a wooden spoon. When cold and crisp, slip the brandy snaps off the handles and store in an airtight container until ready to serve with the custards.

Crème Brûlée

with Lemon & Lime Shorties

Serves 6

2½ cups heavy cream
1 vanilla bean, split
6 egg yolks
3 tablespoons granulated sugar
1⅓ cups confectioners' sugar, sifted

For the shorties
1 cup all-purpose flour, plus extra for
   dusting
6 tablespoons cornstarch
¼ cup granulated sugar
Grated zest of 1 lemon and 1 lime
1 stick (8 tablespoons) unsalted butter

1 Preheat the oven to 300°F. Heat the cream with the vanilla bean until it reaches boiling point. Whisk the egg yolks and granulated sugar together in a bowl, then pour the mixture over the hot cream.

2 Stir the mixture over a low heat until it thickens enough to coat the back of a wooden spoon. Strain into a small pitcher, then pour into 6 ramekins.

3 Stand the ramekins in a roasting pan half-full of water and bake for 1 hour. Let cool, then chill for at least 3 hours. Just before serving, preheat the broiler. Dust thickly with the confectioners' sugar. Put the ramekins under the hot broiler for 3–4 minutes until the sugar caramelizes. Let chill for 30 minutes.

4 Make dough for the shorties while the crèmes brûlées are baking. Preheat the oven to 325°F. Mix the flour, cornstarch, sugar, and lemon and lime zests together in a bowl. Add the butter and rub it in until the mixture resembles bread crumbs. Bring the crumbs together to form a smooth ball. Roll the dough out onto a lightly floured surface and stamp out 12–14 rounds with a 3-inch biscuit cutter.

5 Put on a nonstick baking sheet and bake for 20 minutes, or until golden brown. Let cool until crisp, then store in an airtight container until ready to serve.

Crêpes Suzette

Makes eight 8-inch pancakes

1 cup all-purpose flour
Pinch of salt
2 medium eggs, beaten
1¼ cups milk
Zest of 1 orange
1 tablespoon granulated sugar
Vegetable oil, for frying

To serve
Zest of 1 orange
Zest of 1 lemon
1 tablespoon granulated sugar
⅔ cup orange juice
⅓ stick (3 tablespoons) unsalted butter
3 tablespoons Cointreau

1 Sift the flour and salt into a mixing bowl. Add the eggs and half the milk. Whisk until thick and smooth. Gradually whisk in the remaining milk until you have a smooth batter the consistency of light cream. Add the orange zest and sugar and mix. Cover and let stand for 20–30 minutes.

2 Lightly oil an 8-inch crêpe pan or skillet. Put the pan over a medium heat. Pour in about 2 tablespoons of the batter and swirl the pan to coat the base thinly and evenly. Cook for about 1 minute until the edges appear dry, then carefully flip or turn the pancake, allowing it to cook on the other side for about 30 seconds. Repeat with remaining batter, stacking pancakes between sheets of paper towels as you go and keeping them warm until ready to serve.

3 To serve, mix the citrus zest, sugar, and orange juice together. Heat a large skillet and add the butter. When melted and foaming, add the juice mixture and bring to a boil for 1–2 minutes until slightly thickened. Fold the pancakes into triangles and add to the pan to heat through. Pour over the liqueur and set alight. Serve once the flames have subsided.

Tip
You can use any other orange liqueur, if you like. These pancakes are wonderful served with cream.

Hazelnut Meringue Cake

Serves 6–8

Butter, for greasing
4 egg whites
1 cup granulated sugar
1 teaspoon pure vanilla extract
1 teaspoon cider vinegar
1 teaspoon cornstarch
2/3 cup toasted hazelnuts, finely ground
2 tablespoons coarsely chopped
   toasted hazelnuts

For the filling

1/3 cup plain yogurt
2 tablespoons whiskey
2 tablespoons honey
1/2 cup heavy or whipping cream
1 pint fresh raspberries
Confectioners' sugar, for dusting

1   Preheat the oven to 350°F. Grease and line two 8-inch round cake pans with parchment paper.

2   For the meringue, beat the egg whites in a clean bowl until stiff peaks form. Gradually beat in the sugar to make a stiff and glossy meringue. Fold in the vanilla extract, vinegar, cornstarch, and ground hazelnuts.

3   Divide the mixture evenly between the two prepared pans and level the surface. Scatter the chopped hazelnuts over the top of one, then bake in the oven for 50–60 minutes, or until crisp. Turn out on to a wire rack and let cool.

4   For the filling, stir the yogurt, whiskey, and honey together in a bowl. Whip the cream in a separate bowl until soft peaks form, then fold into the yogurt mixture together with the raspberries.

5   Sandwich the two meringues together with the cream mixture, with the nut-topped meringue uppermost. Dust with confectioners' sugar and serve in slices.

Index